T0161237

THE FIRST 25 YEARS

Edited by Betsy Wakefield Teter

Copyright©2020
Hub City Press

First printing, September 2020

Editor: Betsy Wakefield Teter
Cover design: Meg Reid and Brandy Lindsey & The Graphics House
Interior design: Brandy Lindsey & The Graphics House
Proofreaders: Susan Baker, Bea Bruce, and Leslie Sainz
Printed in the United States

A small portion of Liner Notes is excerpted from "Saving Place," Utne Reader, Sept-Oct 1998

Photo credits:
Rebecca Arrowood – 106 (Diane Chamberlain)
Clay Bolt – 88 (fox)
Kavin Bradner – 98
Chandler Crawford – 81
Carroll Foster – 16, 17, 36, 38, 70, 71, 74, 76, 84, 89 (sculpture), 92, 100, 102, 104, 107 (Victor La Valle), 126
Andrew Green – 20
Carmela Henderson – 13
John Lane – 120 (bottom left)
Stephen Long – 14, 15, 58, 62, 69, 78
Kari Jackson Mailloux – 69
Rob McDonald – 96, 97
Mark Olencki – 11, 12, 13, 24, 26, 30, 32, 34, 42, 44, 60
Zack Parks – 118
S.A. Rankin – 120 (bottom right)
Meg Reid – 90, 106 (David Joy), 110, 116, 122, 124, 132, 133, 134
Spartanburg Herald Journal and GoUpstate – 54, 56, 123
Betsy Teter – 18, 70, 106 (Chaser), 129 (top)
Nick Trainor - 10
Utne Reader - 8
Stewart Winslow - 72

Library of Congress Cataloging-in-Publication Data pending
ISBN: 978-1-938235-73-3

200 Ezell Street
Spartanburg SC 29306
hubcity.org

*Dedicated to the one thousand writers whose work has appeared in a Hub City book
and to all those who have served as board members, staff, and volunteers*

THE HUB CITY WRITERS PROJECT THANKS ITS FRIENDS WHO MADE CONTRIBUTIONS IN SUPPORT OF THIS BOOK AND OTHER HUB CITY PROGRAMS.

William Faulkner Society
$10,000 and up
Valerie & Bill Barnet
Chapman Cultural Center
Mimi Wyche & Davis Enloe
Katherine & Charles Frazier
The National Endowment for the Arts
Agnes & Bill Peelle
Michel & Eliot Stone
J M Smith Foundation
South Carolina Arts Commission

Zora Neale Hurston Society
$5,000 to $9,999
Amazon Literary Partnership
Balmer Foundation
Marshall Chapman
John & Kirsten Cribb
Humanities SC
Susu & George Dean Johnson Jr.
Betsy Teter & John Lane
Milliken & Company
Deborah McAbee & Byron Morris

Flannery O'Connor Society
$1,000 to $4,999
Patty & C. Mack Amick
Paula & Stan Baker
Susan Bridges
Carolina Alliance Bank
Lacy Chapman
Stephen Colyer
Michele & Halsey Cook
Carol & Edwin Epps
Exxon Mobil Foundation
The Graphics House
Ann & Stewart Johnson
Dorothy & Julian Josey
Sara & Paul Lehner
Gayle Magruder
Maggie Miller
Weston Milliken
Carlin & Sander Morrison
Mary Ann Claud & Olin Sansbury
Betty Snow
Sally & Warwick Spencer
Jenny & Ben Stevens
Katherine Wakefield
Catherine Woodard

Eudora Welty Society
$500 to $999
Greg & Lisa Atkins
Arkwright Foundation
Linda & Vic Bilanchone
Bea Bruce
Colonial Trust Company
Nancy & Paul Coté
Tom Moore Craig
Magruder H. Dent
Gail & Chris Ebert
Wendy King & Dan Ebin
Jo & Bob Hackl
Susan Hamilton
Francois Laroche & Jeffrey Herrick
Susan & Ralph Hilsman
Janice & Richard Howerton
Nancy Tiller & Chip Johnson
Nancy Kenney
Leigh Anne & T. Ryan Langley
Nan & Tom McDaniel
Diana D. McGraw
Karen & Bob Mitchell
Erin Ouzts
Mary and Andy Poliakoff
Julian & Beverly Reed
Melissa Walker & Chuck Reback
Betsy & Ricky Richardson
Diane Vecchio & John Stockwell
William Webster
Alanna & Don Wildman
Dennis & Annemarie Wiseman

Friends
$100 to $499
Betsy Adams
Heather & Winthrop Allen
Sarah & Mitch Allen
Ruta Allen
Ceci & Tom Arthur
Susan & Robert Atkins
Kitsy & Andrew Babb
Susan Baker
Lynn & Vic Bailey
Georgianna & Harold Ballenger
Joan & Tom Barnet
Laura & John Bauknight
Cyndi & David Beacham
Christi & Charles Bebko

Elizabeth D. Bernardin
Teresa Betsill
Lynn & Mark Blackman
June & Glen Boggs
Carol & Jim Bradof
Richard Brown
Christopher Bundy
Alissa Burge
Margaret & Robert Burnette
Katherine & William Burns
Lynne & Bill Burton
Lori & Fritz Butehorn
Judy & Brant Bynum
Toni & Jan Caldwell
Kathy & Marvin Cann
Harriet Cannon
Camilla & Jeff Cantrell
Renee & Jay Cariveau
Isabel Forbes & Beth Cecil
Anne Cecil
Sally & Randall Chambers
Elizabeth Chapman
Nan & Tim Cleveland
Janeen & Robert Cochran
Molly & Gregory Colbath
Douglas Congdon
Sue & Rick Conner
Helen & Ben Correll
Haidee Courson
Ted & Rebecca Daniel
Jed Dearybury
Rachel & Kenneth Deems
Susan & Rick Dent
Alice & Chris Dorrance
Jean Dunbar
Susan Dunlap
Kathy & Ray Dunleavy
Kirsten & Levon Eastin
Alice Eberhardt
Coleman Edmunds
Anne Elliott
Joyce Finkle
Susan & W. Russel Floyd
Lyssa & Eric Foust
Donald L. Fowler
Julia Franks
Elaine T. Freeman
Faith Gaskins
Brandt Goodwin

Elaine & Barney Gosnell
Scott Gould
Andrew Green
Margaret & Chip Green
Cassi Grier
Marianna & Roger Habisreutinger
Kitty & Lee Hagglund
Mary Lib Hamilton
Anita & Al Hammerbeck
Monty Mullen & Julian Hankinson
Emily Harbin
Carolyn & Robert Harbison III
Marie & Rodney Harley
Darryl Harmon
Lou Ann & John Harrill Jr.
Anna Harris-Parker
Frances Hardy
Michele & Peyton Harvey
James Mark Hayes II
Margaret & Warren Hayslip
Nancy Hearon
Rita & David Heatherly
Carmela & Gary Henderson
Araceli Hernandez-Laroche
Ed Hicks
Stephanie Highsmith
Charlie Hodge
Holly Hoenig
Marilyn & Doug Hubbell
Patsy Hudgens
Elsa Hudson
Josephine Hutcheson
Max Hyde
Harriet & David Ike
Susan Hodge Irwin
Anne Chapman & Al Jeter
Melissa & Steve Johnson
Tom Johnson
Wallace Johnson
Betsy & Charles Jones
Frannie Jordan
Cathryn & Michael Judice
Daniel Kahrs
Pam & Jay Kaplan
James Karegeannes
Gibert Kennedy
Beverly Knight
Ruth & Bert Knight
Deborah Kocisko
John M. Kohler, Jr.
Mary Jane & Cecil Lanford
Kay & Jack Lawrence
Ruth & Joe Lesesne
Francie & Lindsay Little
Frances & George Loudon
Elizabeth Lowndes

Mary Speed & Manning Lynch
Nancy & Robert Lyon
Julia Lyons
Kari & Phillip Mailloux
Nancy Mandlove
Timothy Marsh
Jim Mayo
Wendy & Bill Mayrose
Connie McCarley
Judy McCravy
William McCrary Jr.
Rob McDonald
Ray McManus
Molly Talbot-Metz
Larry E. Milan
Mary & Don Miles
Diane Milks
Carole & Boyce Miller
Lynda & Bert Moore
Marsha Moore
Peter Moore
Mamie Morgan
Edna Morris
Susan Griswold & John Morton
Trannie Mosley
Susan Myers
Naomi Richardson
Clare & Kirk Neely
Liz Newall
Margaret & George Nixon
Susan & Walter Novak
Hope Nunnery
Chris Offutt
Mark Olencki
Jane Ovenden
Elliott & Painter, LLP
Hannah Palmer
Louise & Keith Parris
Penni & Steve Patton
Nancy Pemberton
Sara Lynn & Jan Postma
Mamie Potter
Kay & Perrin Powell
Betty Price
Mary Frances Price
Sharon Purvis
Frances & Phillip Racine
Eileen Rampey
Ann & Ron Rash
Allison & John Ratterree
Elizabeth Refshauge
Alix & Luke Refshauge
Naomi Richardson
Rose Mary Ritchie
Elisabeth & Regis Robe
Renee Romberger

Bonnie Ares Royster
Elena Pribyl Rush
Premanjali & Nayef Samhat
Kaye Savage
Katherine Schofield
Kathryn Schwille
Carol & Mark Scott
Molly & Gordon Sherard
Ginger Shuler
George Singleton
Becky & Danny Smith
Karen Smith
Pamela Smith
Carolina & Ron Smith
Emily Louise Smith
Chris Smutzer
Rita & Eugene Spiess
Tracy & Russ Stapleton
Brad Steinecke
Mary & Tommy Stokes
Tammy & David Stokes
Brenda & Ed Story
Margaret Sullivan
Christine & Bob Swager
Merike Tamm
Pat & John Tatham
Nancy D. Taylor
Cathy Terrell
Frank Thies III
Mary Ann Thornton
Joan Tobey
Kim & Aaron Toler
Abby Travis
Malinda & Charles Tulloh
Gloria Underwood
Meredith & Mark Van Geison
Judith Waddell
Winnie & Bill Walsh
Jerri & Lawrence Warren
Jennifer Washburn
Anne & Andrew Waters
Mary Ellen Wegrzyn
Kathie & Peter Weisman
Brian Welsch
Cathy & Andy Westbrook
Linda & Dave Whisnant
Ruth Cate & Chuck White
Karen & John B. White Jr.
Cecelia & Nick Wildrick
Floride & William Willard
Elizabeth "Libbo" Wise
Brad Wright
Diane Smock & Brad Wyche
Carolyn & Bob Wynn
Julia Young

LINER NOTES
Betsy Teter

THERE WAS ONLY SUPPOSED TO BE ONE BOOK. On a morning in May 1995, three writers sat in the window of a coffee shop and drew a plan on a napkin to enlist others to write about the experience of living in Spartanburg, an old cotton mill town struggling to find its new identity. We chose a name, Hub City Writers Project, that conjured an earlier Spartanburg railroad heyday and evoked the bold spirit of President Franklin D. Roosevelt's Depression-era Federal Writers Project. As we sipped our cups of Blue Ridge Blend at the little table overlooking the abandoned town-square-turned-parking-lot, we talked about how writers—and this one book—could potentially lift our battered city from its spiritual and economic doldrums.

It was a dream both modest and wildly ambitious.

Little did we know that twenty-five years later the Hub City Writers Project would publish its 100th book, the one you hold, and that our fledgling enterprise would one day publish one thousand writers and counting. We could not have

>>>

known that in the future there would be ten people on the Hub City payroll, serving readers and writers locally and afar. Or that our books would be reviewed in top newspapers and magazines from coast to coast. Or that we would renovate two decrepit buildings on the western end of downtown, one in 2006 and one in 2010, paving the way for a robust area that became known as the Grain District, now home to a luxury hotel, restaurants, and a brewery. We could not have known that our work would twice receive the top arts honor in South Carolina. Or that young writers from Seattle to Texas to New England soon would come live in Spartanburg as part of our national residency program. Little did we know that we would forge a path that other budding publishers around the country would emulate. Or that we would create a roadmap to show other literary non-profits how to open independent bookstores. As John Lane, Gary Henderson,

and I added names of fifteen potential writers for the *Hub City Anthology* to our list, we just hoped we could pull off the publication of one book.

In truth, this is one of the unlikeliest of literary success stories, unfolding as it did in a place with no writers of note to inspire us and no big university budget or giant hometown corporate foundation to fund us. Our ongoing success is somehow intrinsic to the gritty community itself, fueled by a city committed to outrunning economic collapse. One hundred local donors in 1995 have become five hundred donors in 2020. And as the three Hub City founders step to the sidelines, a new generation of literary publishers and programmers have taken the wheel—most in their twenties and thirties, moving here from Canada, Miami, Atlanta, North Carolina, and elsewhere. Their new energy has put the Hub City Writers Project into elite company, among the country's fine independent presses and literary organizations receiving funding from the National Endowment for the Arts, Amazon Literary Partnership, and Charles Frazier's Cold Mountain Fund.

From the very beginning, poet John Lane was "the vision guy." In the late 1970s, before coming home to join the English faculty at Wofford College, John had worked in Port Townsend, Washington, alongside Sam Hamill and Tree Swenson at the

Downtown Spartanburg, early 1990s: Magnolia Street in the foreground, Cleveland Hotel and Spartan Grain in back.

legendary poetry publisher Copper Canyon Press. There, he was immersed in the West Coast's emerging bioregional movement. Bioregionalists focus their advocacy on distinct geographic and ecological places. "I didn't realize it right away, but moving to Port Townsend had landed me in the middle of the intellectual and practical rethinking of the way we inhabit places, a project that would, years later, change the way I looked at my hometown of Spartanburg, and possibly even change the way it looked at itself," he later wrote in an essay for the book *The Bioregional Imagination: Literature, Ecology, and Place*. John also brought back an idea he took from California's Black Sparrow Press: we could fund our *Hub City Anthology* by soliciting one-hundred-dollar sponsors who would receive a limited-edition hardback and have their names appear in the list of donors at the front of the book.

Gary Henderson, a decade older than John and me, brought historical context and a remarkable memory of the city's past to the group. A fine writer and journalist then working for the Spartanburg *Herald-Journal*, Gary remembered when Main Street thrived. He had been a teenager in the 1950s when downtown Spartanburg was filled with department stores, movie theaters, and hotels. But shopping malls on the outskirts of town had stripped the city of its vitality—most downtown buildings in the 1990s were empty, underused, or destined for the wrecking ball. Gary, too, had recently returned from away: Boulder, Colorado, a creative community that valued and protected its beautiful spaces. Gary was particularly pulled toward what was left of Spartanburg's old train depot, the heart of the Hub City, a place where seven rail lines once crossed. As plans came together for the book, Gary took on arrangements for a launch party amid the ruins of the once grand train station.

L to R: Gary Henderson, Betsy Teter, John Lane

Me? I was the Buick dealer's daughter who headed not into the family company, but into journalism, spending eight years as business editor and columnist for my hometown Spartanburg newspaper, becoming immersed in audacious ideas for the future of our community and pestering its leaders about solving our problems. As a child, I had grown up at a local private school and a country club; needless to say, by my mid-thirties, I was *connected*. I also apparently had a latent sales and marketing gene that would click into place when we pulled the first case of Hub City books off the back of an eighteen-wheeler. All that, plus being a history major and a fervent fiction reader, meant I was born to be the first executive director of the Hub City Writers Project.

Which, two years later, would pay me the grand annual sum of $10,000.

The original Hub City writers included teachers, journalists, fiction writers, and poets. One was a retired textile executive, another was a radio commentator, another a transplanted columnist for a major Midwestern newspaper. They were Black

and white, young and old, native and newcomer. As their *Hub City Anthology* essays came in, we realized that this collection of voices had defined Spartanburg in a way it had never been defined before. Through personal stories of the seemingly mundane, a place had emerged—a place that was sad, proud, and a bit eccentric. There were stories about the county fair, a Greek family reunion, back porches, life in the suburbs, kites, a stray cat, and, yes, of course, trains. Later in the process we decided to invite artists and photographers to our book. John's good friend Mark Olencki took on the design work.

On the afternoon of April 23, 1996, thirty writers and artists huddled on the train platform dodging a light drizzle. We had food and drink and books on hand for the three hundred guests we hoped would show up. We were completely unprepared for what happened next. People began coming from everywhere, tying up traffic in three directions, filling every parking lot up and down Magnolia Street. As they waited in line to have authors sign their books, they spilled out onto the tracks, sipping wine and chatting with their neighbors, prompting a visit by a surly railroad detective who warned that if we didn't get the crowd under control he would shut us down. Boxes of new books emptied, and we made a mad dash to Olencki Graphics for more. When the event was over two hours later, the police estimated that as many as fifteen hundred people had come to buy our books and be part of the celebration. Even now, twenty-five years later, that represents the single largest book signing in the history of the Hub City Writers Project.

That kind of success seemed to demand another Spartanburg book. And another. And another. And another. We formed a board of directors in 1997 and began working our way toward becoming an official non-profit organization. Pre-Amazon, pre-distributor, we sold books out of the backs of our cars, shopping them to Spartanburg's four bookstores, to beauty salons, hardware stores, fruit stands, and men's clothing shops. The outside world began to take notice. I was invited to write an article about Hub City for *Orion Afield*, a small Massachusetts magazine focused on grassroots activity. It got republished in *Utne Reader* and mailed to its quarter of a million subscribers. Calls came in from across the country. Could we help them create a Writers Project in their hometowns? The editor of a North Carolina magazine called *Brightleaf* came to Spartanburg to write a story about us; he left flabbergasted that a group of writers had somehow amassed a bank account of $50,000 producing local books.

Opposite page: Contributors to Hub City Anthology. *Above, clockwise: David Taylor, Cooper Smith, Butler Brewton (seated), Max Goldberg (standing), signing outside Pic-A-Book, 1996; Pat Jobe, Meg Barnhouse, Gary Henderson, John Lane and Betsy Teter at Hub City billboard, 1998;* Hub City Christmas *authors at Westgate Mall signing, 1998: Gene Lassiter, Mike Hembree, Elaine Lang Ferguson, Betsy Teter, Gloria Underwood, Marc Henderson, Gary Henderson, Meg Barnhouse; map of essays in* Hub City Anthology.

We may have had some money in the bank, but we were a shoestring operation at best. The office was my cluttered dining room table on Palmetto Street. There was a fax machine in my bedroom upstairs, which invariably rang at 4 a.m. with a Baker & Taylor order for one copy of *Seeing Spartanburg*. We still met regularly for morning coffee and brainstorming, but by then, the short-lived Morgan Square Coffee had been reborn as the more plebeian Sandwich Factory. Hub City's book inventory was spread all over town in closet-sized self-storage units. Our little board of directors held a strategic planning session at nearby Lake Summit; when asked where we saw Hub City going in the future, artist Dorothy Josey drew a picture of a cute storefront with flowerpots outside.

"Well, that'll never happen," I whispered to John, rolling my eyes.

Along the way, though, we'd made quite a splash in our hometown. We held a huge concert to launch a book about Spartanburg musicians. People stood outside the 1,400-seat auditorium with signs saying, "Need tickets." We threw an environmental arts festival to launch a book about Spartanburg's Lawson's Fork Creek, packing a moving van with art canoes, music equipment, tents, and books for four days of events in communities along the river; hundreds of adults and children joined in. We commissioned public art. We built a paddling trail. We started a reading series at the now-renovated train depot. The newspaper hired us to write a serial mystery. The hospital asked us to contribute poetry for their emergency room walls. Other local businesses sprang up using the Hub City moniker. There was a sense that we were becoming beloved.

In the summer of 2001 we actually got our first office, a free space on the fifth floor of the crumbling, half-dark Montgomery Building downtown. There was just enough room for two desks, and I hired my first part-time assistant. That year marked our first foray outside Spartanburg, too. In a partnership with the state Arts Commission in Columbia, we published an anthology of top

The 2nd floor of the HUB-BUB Building housed the Showroom and offices. Four artists-in-residence lived above.

South Carolina fiction writers. We were no longer just a local publisher—we were a *statewide* publisher. The next year, at the tender age of seven, we collected one of those coveted, hefty statuettes called the Elizabeth O'Neill Verner Governor's Award for the Arts in a ceremony inside the South Carolina House of Representatives.

In the fall of 2004 a momentous call came in from the Spartanburg city manager. A branding firm had made an unusual recommendation for a hip entertainment website called HUB-BUB.COM as a way to create the appearance that a burgeoning creative class lived here. The perplexed City Council had thrown up its hands. Would the Hub City Writers come take a look at this proposal? You bet, we said. Anything that had HUB in its name should accrue to us. We gathered the most creative young minds in Spartanburg, and we countered: Okay, we'll do the website, but we need our own performing arts center and four apartments for an artist-in-residence program.

And thus began the wild HUB-BUB years.

Staffed up with two new full-time employees, the Showroom opened in a former Nash Rambler dealership-turned-overstock-shoe-emporium in the summer of 2006. Situated between a defunct animal feed plant and a concrete-block motorcycle club, our two-story headquarters was a bold proclamation that the arts could help lead Spartanburg's downtown revitalization. Never mind that the police officer who did our first-day inspection suggested we put bars on the windows to keep the criminals out. With a broadened mission statement, the Hub City Writers Project launched into the entertainment business with a full slate of concerts, edgy art shows, independent films, offbeat theatre productions, and, yes, poetry readings. In came the first

The Belleville Outfit warms up in the Hub City office.

group of young artists-in-residence, including one with a five-foot hairy spider with a screaming human head on top. Spartanburg was definitely changing.

Simultaneously, the publishing continued apace, usually four to five books a year. We created an editorial board that included recent transplant C. Michael Curtis, senior editor of *The Atlantic* magazine. We partnered with the Arts Commission to create the South Carolina First Novel Prize, the first of its kind in the country. We signed a contract with rising literary superstar Ron Rash to publish his next poetry book, *Waking*. We rebranded, with a new logo, and officially became Hub City Press. With the help of the city's magnanimous hospitality taxes funding rent on the Showroom, our publishing project weathered the Great Recession, though just barely.

Truth be told, the phenomenal success of HUB-BUB was eclipsing the Hub City Writers Project. We were pushed into a back corner of an office that doubled as a green room, and we'd run out of wall space for our books. A glass-front room originally

The Hub City Bookshop has become an important gathering place for Spartanburg.

intended as a little bookstore instead had become a closet for stacks of blue plastic Showroom chairs. Our dream of being a literary town was buried under rock 'n' roll bands, naughty Christmas plays, and skateboard art. We began to think that maybe it was time for another brainstorm.

After months of furious fundraising and construction, the Hub City Bookshop and Press headquarters opened in summer 2010 a block away from the Showroom on the ground floor of the historic Masonic Temple. Joining us there were two other start-ups, a coffee shop (of course) and a micro-bakery. This momentous occasion called for a good, old fashioned Hub City street party. We invited two bands, set up antique typewriters on the sidewalk to collect our guests' good wishes, hauled in an old refrigerator for magnetic poetry games, and peddled books, coffee, and cupcakes as a thousand happy Spartans celebrated in the street. City Council came. The Masons came. Even a flash mob came. John, Gary, and I stood together on the edge of the crowd and marveled at how far we'd come.

We now had Dorothy's cute little storefront, complete with a flowerpot outside.

The Masonic Temple quickly became Spartanburg's left bank, a place where intellectuals, artists, activists, and avid readers found a home. Businesspeople and politicians in suits soon followed. Most mornings, every outdoor café table under the Temple's monumental copper awning was filled. In the evenings we hosted readings, spelling bees, and game nights. Each January, Virginia the Airedale terrier and her human friends, all wearing party hats, showed up for a doggie birthday celebration outside. Writers passing through town began to stop in, and the guest book at the front door filled up with the names of book browsers from hundreds of miles away.

The opening of our bookstore marked the first time that any literary non-profit in the United States had opened a full-service independent bookstore, but it wouldn't be the last. During the next decade, others followed in Minneapolis, Winston-Salem, Chicago, and Tulsa. Did we know what we were doing? Not really. But we had dealt with enough indie bookstores over the years to have a hunch.

It was immediately clear how good an idea this was. Book sales were so unexpectedly strong that they funded a full-time assistant press director position, filled first by Kari Jackson, then by Meg Reid, then, as the staff grew again, by Kate McMullen. Anne Waters, the former president of the Publishing Association of the South, arrived in town in 2013, assumed the bookstore manager's job, and eventually became our second executive director. We added an outreach coordinator, Leslie Sainz; an inventory manager, Lee Holden; an events manager and booksellers. In an initiative called Growing Great

Readers, we gave away tens of thousands of summer reading books to elementary school children in disadvantaged local neighborhoods. Budding booksellers from hundreds of miles away made pilgrimages to Spartanburg to learn how to recreate the Hub City Bookshop in their own communities.

Outside the store, we worked with city officials to build a shady pocket park adjacent to the Masonic Temple. We created the Spartanburg Music Trail, sixteen placards around town that honored the musicians spotlighted in our 1997 *Hub City Music Makers* book. Buildings went up around us—tall ones—and

sidewalks filled with people returning downtown. Improbably, I got named Tourism Person of the Year by the Chamber of Commerce.

Meanwhile, the fortunes of Hub City Press soared. We published our first book by a non-South Carolinian in 2010. A year later, there was an anthology of African-American poets from across both Carolinas, edited by Kwame Dawes. It was time for a change in mission again: Hub City Press was now focused on publishing "new and extraordinary writers from the American South." Our stable of writers swelled to include poets,

These are some of the titles published by Hub City Press 2017-2019.

The Hub City Bookshop celebrated its tenth birthday on June 30, 2020.

memoirists, and fiction writers from Virginia, Alabama, Texas, Tennessee, North Carolina, Kentucky, West Virginia, and beyond. All of a sudden, there was a cluster of five Hub City authors in Atlanta. With Meg Reid's creative eye, we became known for our outstanding book design. James McTeer's novel, *Minnow*, was a Kirkus Book of the Year. Julia Franks' novel, *Over the Plain Houses*, was an NPR Book of the Year and won a host of other literary prizes. IPPY Awards—twenty-two so far—piled up. The premier independent book distributor in the country, Publishers Group West, invited us to come on board, and suddenly our staff was flying off to San Francisco for sales conferences. Seasoned sales reps began pitching our titles at national gatherings of booksellers and librarians. In April 2020, Southern lifestyle magazine *Garden and Gun* named Anne, Meg, and me among thirty people "saving the South" in an issue about the region's cultural heroes. "People are saying y'all are the new Algonquin," Ron Rash said to me at a book conference, referring to the powerhouse Southern publisher that rose up in Chapel Hill in 1983.

In recent years we have headed off into incredible new directions that readers and supporters in Spartanburg may not even be aware of. And so it is time to celebrate with a special book that captures the high points of the Hub City Writers Project history, complete with photos, illustrations, and memorabilia. If the cover of this book looks familiar, that's on purpose. It takes as its inspiration the hometown Marshall Tucker Band's *Greatest Hits* album of 1978. Many of the Hub City stars of the past have returned to tell their little pieces of the larger story, to create our own Greatest Hits. We salute them and the hundreds of other Hub City writers whose names appear at the back.

Here's to the next twenty-five years!

THE OFFICE ON MORGAN SQUARE
John Lane

Blueberry muffins weren't the only thing cooked up at Gary Koch's Morgan Square Coffee when the Californian opened it at 137 West Main Street in 1994. Soon after, a group of new friends with literary aspirations—two journalists, Betsy and Gary Henderson, and me, a poet—began meeting mornings there. A round marble-top table and a circle of chairs became an unexpected particle accelerator to change Spartanburg one story at a time.

The swirling energy of friendship and humor pulled others in. There was Meg, the college chaplain with a sharp wit; Mack, a retired Navy nurse; Mark, the photographer; and David, the young English professor, among others.

Before long Gary Koch moved on, and the California coffee shop became Jack Dunsmore's Sandwich Factory, a combo breakfast-lunch spot with good coffee and great turkey Reuben sandwiches. Later Bill Roach ran it as the Café on Morgan Square. Through the years, each weekday morning, we continued our conversations in what became our defacto office. We voiced a desire for our community. We wanted to tell stories that would define the particular outline of a community in distress, for Spartanburg in those early days lacked a focus.

A morning gathering at the "center of the universe"

What pushed us beyond the outlines of any community coffee klatch was that the creative ferment did not merely swirl restlessly about. We harnessed that morning mayhem. By the time the café closed in 2011, more than forty books had been produced. We had a real office by then, but the Hub City founders and friends continued to hold court there until the bitter end. We came for conversation and friendship. When the end finally came, what we carried away was a legacy.

COMING SOON . . .

"The Hub City Anthology:

Spartanburg Writers & Artists"

1

**HERE'S HOW TO OWN
ONE OF 100
LIMITED EDITION,
HARD COVER BOOKS**

THE FIRST LOGO for the Hub City Writers Project lasted about two weeks. To raise money for the first book in fall 1995, Betsy Teter made a brochure with clip-art (1), Scotch tape, and horrible orange copier paper. Some of those fliers actually went out in the mail. John Lane grimaced, said, "Wait a minute," and called his designer pal Mark Olencki for a drink. Mark flipped over a beer coaster and began sketching (2). Within minutes, there was a logo, a real logo (3), one that lasted us more than ten years and adorned sweatshirts, posters, hats, stickers, and more. But it didn't work particularly well for book spines. The first three Hub City books came out under the imprint of John's micro-publishing venture, Holocene (4), and so their spines carried its artful "h" logo (also created by Mark). By the fourth book, Mark had created a spine logo for us that evoked the famous LOVE sculpture in New York City (5). In 2010, when we opened the Hub City Bookshop, it was time for a new logo. Stephen Long created one inspired by Frank Lloyd Wright's bold geometric design (6). We use it in orange for the bookshop, green for the press, and blue for the writers project.

2

3

5

 Holocene

4

6

THE LAUNCH
Gary Henderson

From the beginning, the Hub City Writers Project has surprised us. Neither Betsy Teter, John Lane, nor I imagined when *Hub City Anthology*, our first book, debuted we'd be writing stories for a twenty-fifth anniversary publication. Yet, here we are, and what an honor.

Looking back, there were hints in the tea leaves. We expected maybe three hundred people might respond to our promotions for the book launch event at the old train depot downtown in April 1996. On noon newscasts we filled the television airwaves with Betsy on Channel 7 and me on Channel 4. Add print, radio, and personal appearances, and the stage was set for Spartanburg literary history.

Shortly after the five o'clock p.m. start time it was clear that what we thought was a generous hope for crowd size was a drastic underestimation. Before the evening was over, some fifteen hundred people pored through the pages of our anthology of Spartanburg writers, artists, and photographers.

One of them, a thirteen-year-old boy, stopped in front of me and pushed his copy of the anthology across the table for me to autograph. "I want to be a writer too," he said as he watched me sign my name on the title page of "Jack's Kite," the essay I wrote for the book. He told me how he practiced writing and loved when he had writing assignments in school.

Those of us whose work appeared in the anthology signed books for three hours that night and sent nearly eight hundred copies of the book home in the hands of readers. The boy I met the night of the release party would be thirty-eight years old now. I hope he realized his dreams to be a writer and felt the pride an author experiences seeing his name on the cover of a book. It's a pleasure Hub City Writers Project has made possible for hundreds of writers. I am honored to have been one of them.

HUB CITY MUSIC MAKERS
Peter Cooper

I was teaching middle school in Rock Hill, my days spent in the classroom, my early evenings spent lesson planning, and my late nights spent pondering the foolhardy decisions that led me to teach middle school in Rock Hill. Betsy Teter and John Lane threw me a lifeline in the form of an idea that seemed daunting and audacious to me, and silly to most everyone outside of a small circle of visionary Spartans.

"You're writing a history of Spartanburg music? That'll make for a good pamphlet."

But they had no idea. Most of Spartanburg had no idea. I had no idea, until I dove in. I knew pieces of the story but didn't understand the enormity of the thing … the geniuses of blues, country, rock, folk, gospel, and classical music whose common grounds were Pine Street, Asheville Highway, and Cannons Campground Road. They all shared grit and virtuosity, and most of them had a queasy relationship with Spartanburg: they and the city were middle schoolers eyeing each other questioningly at the dance.

With Betsy playing no-nonsense coach Vince Lombardi and John serving as the literary version of happy cloud painter Bob Ross, I finished the book, and it served to awaken people to the gifts in their midst. And then we threw a concert, filling the Twichell Auditorium stage with people who had performed all over the world and with people who spent most weekends playing in front of TVs and pool tables.

Eastside bluebloods and westside rowdies, white folks and black folks … everyone joined in a celebration in which the power of music triumphed over grudges and misunderstandings, and even over Spartanburg's long-held inferiority complex. Music pointed the way to appreciation, reconciliation, and revitalization. And now I don't have to teach middle school.

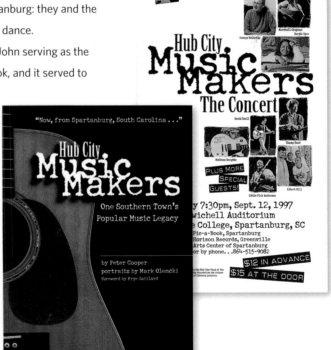

BUBBAS ON PARADE
Meg Barnhouse

Writers never expect to be asked to be Grand Marshals of a parade. Parades are exuberant outdoor activities and writing is a quiet, indoor one. Shortly after the release of *The Best of Radio Free Bubba* in 1998, a small country town wanted to celebrate the new identity Hub City was giving the area. We were becoming a hotbed of literary and artistic creativity. I'm guessing even the kids got involved with parade prep, given that the sign on the side of our car said *GRANAD MASHALS HUB CITY WITERERS*.

We were trying to be cool. Practicing our waves as we waited to get into the parade car, we kept our ironic remove. For a while. It was a parade, though, and ironic remove is hard to maintain to the music of a marching band, especially when you're sitting up on the backseat of a shiny red car. People waved at us as we rode by. Everyone was smiling. We were too.

It has been important to me to have been part of the birth of Hub City, to see pride growing in an area that suffered so many blows. When people have something to be proud of we hold our heads up. When we hold our heads up we see everything more clearly. Hub City changed our sense of who we were. We were a town of writers, artists, and creatives. I've carried that identity with me even though I live far away these days. I'm a writer. That makes me smile. If you wave to me, I'll wave to you.

The Best of Radio Free Bubba and its 2006 follow-up, *The Return of Radio Free Bubba*, are collections of radio commentaries that originally aired on WNCW, a public radio station in Spindale, NC.

Facing page: Pat Jobe, Meg Barnhouse. Below: Gary Henderson, John Lane, Pat Jobe

"I'm happy when a real quality piece comes from someone who is basically selling books out of the trunks of cars."

–JIM BARNES, ASSOCIATE PUBLISHER OF INDEPENDENT PUBLISHER MAGAZINE

NEW SOUTHERN HARMONIES
George Singleton

On October 5, 1997 I responded to a query from John Lane and Betsy Teter about *New Southern Harmonies*, the anthology of short stories they wished to publish. I was thirty-nine years old and understood that a promise I made to myself—to publish a collection of my own by the age of forty, or flat-out quit this cursed vice—wasn't going to happen. I thought, well, for the rest of my life at least I can flaunt a nice hardcover book with three stories of mine included, along with those of also-bookless-at-the-time Scott Gould, Rosa Shand, and Deno Trakas. So eager was I, I sent something like twenty short stories for consideration—some of them published, most not—to John and Betsy. In the cover letter I mentioned how, if these stories didn't work, then I had another, oh, hundred as-yet-unpublished stories from which to choose, that it wouldn't hurt my feelings (though it would, of course) if none of the stories worked out for the project.

I wrote this letter on a nice Smith-Corona electric typewriter, if it matters.

I guess they felt sorry for me. It happens to thirty-nine-year-old writers shooting buckshot in the air, hoping to hit anything.

I'll jump ahead. *New Southern Harmonies: Four Emerging Fiction Writers* appeared on January 1, 1998. I think I can speak for Scott, Rosa, and Deno when I say we felt a giddiness unknown to most South Carolinians, writers or not. We underwent "book tours," and signed copies, and relished the over-the-top newspaper reviews. The collection won an award.

Listen, this publication might've kept me writing, I guess, and it probably did for my cohorts. I turned forty, forty-one, forty-two, and then ... and then ....

Hub City's first fiction publication won an IPPY Medal as the best short story collection by an independent press in North America. George now has eleven books.

Facing page, L to R: Scott Gould, Rosa Shand, George Singleton, Deno Trakas

David Taylor at Whitney Dam

LAWSON'S FORK, THE BOOK
David Taylor

A river isn't only water—it's topography, geology, plants, animals below and above the surface; a river is also about people. *The Lawson's Fork: Headwaters to Confluence* is no different—it was dreamed up in a coffeehouse conversation, carried along by paddling trips with friends back when folks thought of Lawson's Fork as the toxic drainage ditch running through town. The book is a single stream made by a watershed of contributions, my narrative, John and Betsy's research, Gary Henderson's interviews, Helen Correll's pen and ink drawings, Mark Olencki's photography, and poetry by children and adults influenced by the river. I like to think Lawson's Fork told its story too.

For the river to tell its story, I had to walk it, paddle it, even immerse and baptize myself in it. John Lane and I walked the first trickles of the headwaters through neighborhoods and pastures. We organized a group paddling trip from Whitney Dam to the takeout at Sydnor Road. I lost count of the number of solo trips that ended at the confluence with the Pacolet by Goldmine Road. I needed to read what the scientists were saying about its health and future. Then, I needed to leave the readings, journal, and notes behind and just listen.

Lawson's Fork set the compass for my life's work. Every job I've had and every book I've written since has come from that experience twenty-five years ago—trying to recapture that conversation among place, people, and a more educated and respectful way of getting by. We need myths that bind us to the practice of saving a place, but those myths have to be driven first by encountering and listening to the story that's already and always there.

THE LAWSON'S FORK ENVIRONMENTAL ARTS FESTIVAL
Thomas Pierce

With a grant from the National Endowment for the Arts in hand, Hub City hosted the four-day Environmental Arts Festival in spring 2000 to introduce the Lawson's Fork book and, along the way, created a funky documentary about it.

My buddy and I were two high school juniors whose film CVs mostly included being the youngest members of the movie appreciation club at the Spartanburg Public Library and making mountain biking videos with our friends. But somehow we finagled our way into the local documentary crew that was going to film a four-day festival celebrating Lawson's Fork, the city's long-neglected river. Our job was to interview as many people as we could, which we did, but mostly what I recall now is the two of us geeking out with the camera and doing our best to get what might be generously called unconventional footage. In particular I remember setting up the camera on a tripod, sticking it through the sunroof of a car, and fast-driving the backroads between the festival events because—well, I forget the exact reason, but it had something to do with art. We were making art, and art required spontaneity and experimentation. I'm not sure how much of what we shot wound up in the documentary—that was above our pay-grade—but I do know being a part of that project confirmed for me that if you want to be somebody who *creates*, you can't wait around for it to just happen. If you want to be a filmmaker, you go find a camera and start filming. If you want your town to pay a little more attention to the river at its heart, you organize a festival and celebrate the hell out of it. To me, that's Hub City in a nutshell.

L to R: Robby Cochran (with camera), Thomas Pierce, Gary Henderson

SPARTANBURG IS WAY TOO FASCINATING A PLACE to tell its story in one book. So far, it's taken us thirty-four books … and counting. Over the years there have been books about peach farmers, Revolutionary War battles, noble trees, movie palaces, and popular musicians. There have been two books of Christmas stories, two about local artists, and three about places to eat. We've written about Spartanburg's Greek history and its African-American history. We once gathered forty-six writers to tell our community's textile history. We've told Spartanburg's story through collections of poetry, short stories, and personal essays by local writers. We've covered our city from above, with drone photography (*Above Spartanburg*), and from below (*The Underground Guide to Spartanburg*). By our count, we've sold more than seventy thousand books about Spartanburg. And here's some good news: there are more stories to tell.

"Spartanburg is emphatically the gateway to the Western World."

—*Promotional brochure for Spartanburg, 1888*

LAWSON'S FORK C

ʃEAD WA

ʃVIRONMENTAL ARTS FE

IN THE EARLY DAYS, every book got a t-shirt. On the back we listed the tour dates for book signings, just like the rock bands did. The very first shirt for The Hub City Anthology sported a slogan we found in an 1880 description of Spartanburg: "Emphatically the gateway to the Western World." That hot-seller truly captured our level of ambition. The Radio Free Bubbas got shirts and sold them at their events. The Lawson's Fork shirts were ubiquitous at the Headwaters Environmental Arts Festival. Sometimes the shirts even outsold the books. By about 2001 we realized our wardrobes couldn't keep up with our publishing, and we phased out our line of book apparel. But our old t-shirts live on in the bottom drawers of the early Hub City writers.

The Best of Radio Free BUBBA

Meg Barnhouse-Pat Jo___
Kim Taylor-Gary Phill___

-13 WNCW Fall Fundraiser · Spi___
Sandwich Factory · Spartanbur___
Fireside Books · Forest City, NC
Black Swan Studio · Asheville, N___
Hub City Book & Music Fair · Sp___
Barnes & Noble · Greenville, ___
Open Book · Greenville, SC
Barnes & Noble · Spartanburg, SC___
Cleveland Community College · She___
Malaprop's · Asheville, NC
Angel Shoppe · Asheville, NC

__ba Tour '98

___Cer ___aker The Conc___

HUB CITY writers project

REES Piedmont ___bin

___ND PACKED BY
SPARTANBURG, SOUTH CAROLINA

MARK OLENCKI, THE FIRST DESIGNER
John Lane

For more than a decade, Mark Olencki was the creative heart of the Hub City Writers Project. From the first logo he sketched out on the back of a beer coaster to the first thirty books and beyond, Mark designed everything. Posters. T-Shirts. Brochures. Catalogues. Even a billboard. If literary design ever had a Swiss Army knife, it is Mark.

A photographer by trade, Mark did most of this design work from his studio on South Pine Street. There, he also perfected the art of the literary colophon. Mark's colophons were so stuffed with information at times they felt like mini-memoirs. For those who don't consider themselves connoisseurs of the book arts, a colophon has historically been a statement at the end of a book, typically with a printer's emblem, giving information about its authorship and printing. Usually they name the typefaces used and maybe mention the place and time of the printing. Often they contain the size of the edition. It's said that medieval monks added complaints or even notes of love to their colophons. Mark's colophons have their repeated oddnesses and hilarious surprises as well that I hope some future bibliophile will notice and celebrate. Mark always noted which alcohol— Scotch, beer, or wine— he consumed during the late nights it took to lay out the books; he chronicled which ancient Mac desktop hardware system was still functioning during each book; and finally he noted which version of the bookmaking software Pagemaker, or, in later books, Indesign, magically shaped margins, headers, and photo spreads.

Design is one of the most essential and often overlooked parts of publishing. We were lucky to pull Mark into our community experiment at the very beginning. His stamp on Hub City's success can be seen in so many ways, but one of my favorites is found at the back of those early books.

PIC-A-BOOK
Betsy Teter

Without Jane Hughes and Pic-A-Book, the Hub City Writers Project would have faded within the first year. The quixotic independent bookstore, which reigned on Spartanburg's eastside for thirty-five years, sold thousands of our books. And those books didn't just sell themselves. Jane, who worked seven days a week until she was eighty-five, put them in the hands of most everyone who came in the door. She kept our books on the coveted table next to the entrance. She was always game to host our book signings, sometimes with more than a dozen writers.

Each time Hub City came out with a new Spartanburg book, the first step was to bring a reading copy to the Colonel for his approval. That was Col. John Hughes, who met Jane in the 1940s when he was a soldier training for World War II in Spartanburg. Jane, a registered nurse, had come south from Massachusetts to care for her brother's children while he too trained for combat. They married, and over the decades, a succession of children and grandchildren took their places behind the register in the family business.

Crabbiness was Jane's schtick and she often wore a sweatshirt with the Grinch on the front. When Barnes & Noble opened across town—Jane called it "Butts and Nuts"—she repeatedly threatened to throw our books into the parking lot if I dared supply them. (Full disclosure: I did.) The store itself was a jumble of books. Fiction was filed alphabetically by title rather by than author name. There were piles of books everywhere that Jane handed out free to young readers. Stacks in the back were often full of titles that hadn't sold in a decade. But prosper Pic-A-Book did, by sheer hustle and intense customer loyalty.

When new landlords substantially raised their rent in 2006, the Hughes family decided to end their run. If Hub City had a patron saint in those early years, it was grouchy, generous, wonderful Jane. We owe her immensely.

"During the last twenty-five years, I have watched Hub City grow from a promising vision to become one of our indispensable independent publishers. This dedicated team has made a lasting contribution to the South's, and America's, literature."

Ron Rash in 2001 at Hub City's event, The Woven Word

RON RASH
Betsy Teter

Sometime during the Y2K year, John Lane had another of his brilliant ideas: let's host a reading in Spartanburg for two Carolina poets with new books focused on the textile industry. One was Michael Chitwood of Chapel Hill; the other was a fellow in Clemson named Ron Rash, an English teacher who was holding down a brutal five-course load at Tri-County Technical College. The only problem was that Rash's first poetry book, *Eureka Mill*, had already gone out of print. Its publisher, a small outfit in Columbia, didn't want to do another press run just for our event. "Why don't you guys just take the book?" the publisher said. And so we did. Hub City's edition of *Eureka Mill* appeared in January 2001 with a new cover, just in time for a double-header poetry event we called "The Woven Word."

Little did anyone know we were dealing with a writer who would go on to pen *New York Times* bestsellers, win the Frank O'Connor International Short Story Award, have his books made into movies, and become one of the most cherished and distinguished Southern authors of his generation. Little did we know we had a poetry book that would sell four thousand copies and counting.

A decade later, Rash graciously accepted Hub City's offer to be the publisher of another of his poetry collections, *Waking*, a book termed "wise and wonderful," by Pulitzer Prize-winning poet Claudia Emerson. Over the years, Rash has taught our workshops, blurbed our novels, and given generously to the Hub City Writers Project in so many ways. In 2018, on the 20th anniversary of *Eureka Mill*'s initial publication, we released a new edition of the book with yet another new cover. We got the gang back together and celebrated once again with a Hub City fundraiser at RJ Rockers Brewing Company.

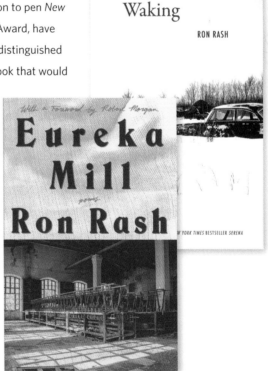

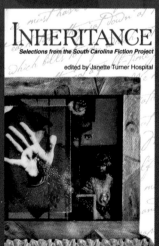

"From their hyper-local, hometown roots, Hub City Writers Project has grown into one of America's best regional publishers. But through every stage of their development and in every smart new enterprise—bookselling, artist residency programs, civic activism—their local terroir has persisted, and I love it. I feel very lucky to have gotten to work with Hub City through a large part of my career at the Arts Commission, and—I can say it now— they've always been one of my favorite organizations! There is nothing quite like them in the state (or maybe anywhere). Here's to the next 25 years!"

-KEN MAY, FORMER DIRECTOR OF THE STATE ARTS COMMISSION

Verner Award ceremony, 2002

PARTNERING WITH THE SOUTH CAROLINA ARTS COMMISSION
Sara June Goldstein

Over twenty years ago, when I was sitting in my Arts Commission office reading through grant applications, I came across a request from the Hub City Writers Project, an organization new to me. I remember how excited I was as I read. So excited—and inspired—that I ran down the hall to ask the director to read the proposal immediately, adding that we *must* support this literary organization. We understood, from that initial encounter, that Hub City was going to be important to artists and audiences in South Carolina. We believed then that Hub City was going to make a difference in the kind of work that the South Carolina Arts Commission could accomplish in literary arts—and we were right.

The Hub City Writers Project, which is now one of the most dynamic and inclusive literary arts organizations in the South, emphasized from the beginning place-based literature that encourages readers to connect more deeply with their communities. About ten years ago, an Arts Commission grant helped them rebrand and publicize their press and programs beyond South Carolina.

In 2002, Hub City received the Elizabeth O'Neill Verner Governor's Award for outstanding contribution to the arts in South Carolina. Hub City was the first literary organization to be honored in the thirty-year history of the awards program. Fifteen years later, in 2017, Betsy Teter, co-founder and executive director of Hub City, received an individual Verner Award for outstanding leadership and achievement in the arts, giving, through Hub City, an innovative literary identity to her state.

Although the Arts Commission partnered with Hub City Writers on many projects, three important book projects would not have been possible without Hub City. The first was a collection of stories from past winners of the South Carolina Fiction Project, *Inheritance*, edited by Janette Turner Hospital. A couple of years later, the Arts Commission worked with Hub City to publish *Twenty*, an anthology of poetry from the S.C. Poetry Fellows, edited by Kwame Dawes. In 2008, the Arts Commission and Hub City partnered with South Carolina Humanities and the SC State Library to produce the biennial South Carolina First Novel Prize (now the South Carolina Novel Prize). My dream come true! Six writers have received the award and the initiative has helped launch writing careers in South Carolina. This is the only novel prize in the nation sponsored by a state Arts Commission.

Thank you, Hub City!

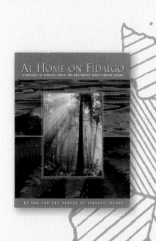

WHO WE INSPIRED

"Inspired by
our visionary
colleagues at the
Hub City Writers Proj-
ect, we asked ourselves: what
are the defining stories at the intersection of
nature and culture in our own bioregion? Fifteen years
later, this anthology is still in print and remains timeless,
binding together a grand store of writers and naturalists in a
purposeful chorus of love and outrage and wisdom."

–SUSAN CERULEAN, EDITOR OF *BETWEEN TWO RIVERS*,
PUBLISHED BY THE RED HILLS WRITERS PROJECT

"Soon after faculty at Franklin Pierce College initiated the Monadnock Institute of Nature, Place and Culture, we began to imagine collecting the stories of our region. We discovered an ideal model for place-based writing in the *Hub City Anthology* published in 1996. (These) stories kindled our inspiration and guided our discussions. Betsy Teter and John Lane became long-distance advisors and mentors for the project we undertook."

–JOHN HARRIS, PROJECTS COORDINATOR, MONADNOCK INSTITUTE

THE STORY OF THE HUB CITY WRITERS PROJECT, published in the national magazines *Orion Afield* and *Utne Reader* in 1998, helped inspire groups of writers from across the country to publish their own books. We call these books "our grandchildren."

At Home on Fidalgo Island (1999)
Fidalgo Island, Washington

The View from Here (2000)
Flagstaff, Arizona

Essence of Beaufort & The Lowcountry (2000)
Beaufort, South Carolina

Between Two Rivers (2004)
The Red Hills region, Florida

Where the Mountain Stands Alone (2006)
The Monadnock region, New Hampshire

Enoree Manufacturing spinners and spoolers, 1896

TEXTILE TOWN
G.C. Waldrep

In 2002, forty-six writers and scholars came together to create Textile Town, *dedicated to the 100,000 men, women, and children who worked in Spartanburg County mills.*

Part of what makes a group of people who live in close proximity to one another a "community" is memory—shared memory. An important part of what *Textile Town* attempted to accomplish was the cultivation of memory as specifically *shared* memory. This is a key way a community recognizes itself and, in recognizing itself, comes into being, as a community.

Visiting Spartanburg regularly in the years since *Textile Town* is bittersweet for me, as the mill-and-village complexes I studied in the mid-1990s fade and disappear. Spartan Mills is gone, and a significant tract of the Spartan village too, to make way for the Northside redevelopment. Arkwright is a ghost town of ruins and weeds; not only are the houses and mill at Crescent Knitting gone, but also the streets themselves, erased from the city map. Saxon, Lyman, Startex, and the Cliftons have lost their mills— and much else besides.

One way to remember, to participate in shared memory, is to have the landscape remember for you. But in the years since *Textile Town,* redevelopment and decay have rooted out much of the industry's trace presence from the landscape itself. One can drive right through Spartanburg from almost any direction now and never know it was a textile town. Language, though, is another way the past leaves traces—which become shared traces when we read. As the poet C.D. Wright asked again and again in her long poem about shared memory and the South, *Deepstep Come Shining,* "now do you know where you are?" I'm glad Hub City took the time to rekindle these shared memories in language before they, too, disappeared.

SOUTH OF MAIN
Brenda Lee Pryce

I grew up in public housing on the Southside of Spartanburg. I always looked forward to running to my grandmother's home at 137 Clement Street to get a cup of sugar or cornmeal, whatever my mom needed to complete her meal for her three children. Stella Cohn's house had a wrap-around porch, and she kept the lawn and hedges manicured. Usually she would be sitting on the porch in her favorite rocking chair. My uncle "Chip" Charlton Cohn served in the Army in WWII and purchased that home for her.

When urban renewal came to my neighborhood in the early 1970s, my grandmother's house was demolished, along with hundreds of others. It broke her heart and mine. Down went most of the Black-owned businesses of the Southside.

When I grew up, I became a community activist, and in 1995 I was the first Black woman from Spartanburg elected to the State Legislature. About that time, I heard about plans to demolish my childhood home, the red brick Tobe Hartwell housing project. I protested loudly and got some people's attention. I had so many good memories there: getting my first pair of Union Hardware skates and skating around the bend backwards; walking to school at Carver High; or seeing Ellen Cheeks, the maid for the Milliken family, in her fur coat, leaving home for church. I was promised they would at least save the historic Tobe Hartwell administration building for posterity, but all of it disappeared.

Beatrice Hill and I often talked about our wonderful memories of growing up on the Southside whenever we would host a Tobe Hartwell reunion. We recorded people's memories and gathered pictures and documents. We brought our collection to the attention of Betsy Teter with the Hub City Writers Project, and the idea for the little black-and-white book called *South of Main* was born. As Spartanburg continues to grow, I pray that city leaders continue to read our book as a reminder of what happens to a community when all voices are not heard. Our city residents should keep a copy of *South of Main* as a reminder of what happens to a community when not all voices are heard.

South of Main, published in 2005, has sold more than 3,700 copies and won the Gold IPPY Medal for best multicultural nonfiction title in North America.

Above: Effie Parks. Facing page: Carrie Nell Wright and Nina Mary Wright, daughters of legendary local educator Mary H. Wright

THE MONTY
Betsy Teter

This piece is from a 2005 blog entry.

Let me tell you about the Montgomery Building, what I call the Third World of Office Buildings, where landlord Arthur Cleveland has graciously allowed us to squat for the past three years. The grand old Montgomery, ten stories tall and solid as an asbestos-covered rock, is in bankruptcy, which I hear is better than foreclosure because the lights and air conditioning stay on (we hope).

It's mostly non-profits now scattered through the halls of the Montgomery—the Cancer Society, the Big Brothers and Big Sisters, some environmentalists, and the Active Living folks next door. (When the elevator shuts down, we all do some active living.) Everyone with means has moved out, rats leaving the proverbial sinking office building. Not too long ago we said good-bye to 96-year-old Mr. Gibson. He had been brokering coal from his office on the fifth floor since the building opened in 1928. Yes, 1928.

We got to keep his hat rack.

We've had some rather sketchy homeless people living on the first floor this month. Their non-profit has fallen on some especially hard times. Not enough people needing drug counseling, or something. A few times a day the woman comes up, borrows our phone, and talks to Momma. She could use a shower, but alas, we don't have that.

The Hub City Writers Project operated out of the Montgomery Building from 2001 to 2006.

The best part of hanging out in the Montgomery Building is the scavenging. Every time someone moves out, we pick up some nice office supplies or furniture. When the printing brokers next door left, we actually tore down the wall with sledge hammers and took their whole office. We have quite the impressive digs up here now, roughly the length of a bowling alley and maybe twice as wide.

There will be plenty more stories about the Montgomery Building on this blog in the coming weeks. Those of us still here are the diehards. As Yon Lambert, my environmentalist buddy upstairs, says, "Hunter Thompson would be proud."

Hub City decamped to the brand new HUB-BUB building in July 2006. The Montgomery was fully renovated in 2019 with new restaurants, apartments, shops, and offices.

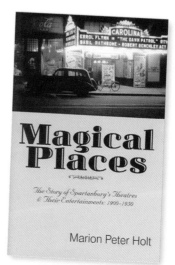

Magical Places

The Story of Spartanburg's Theatres & Their Entertainments: 1900-1950

Marion Peter Holt

THE GREATEST HITS SHOW
Kerry Ferguson

In May 2005, for the tenth anniversary of the press, we gathered together a few talented homegrown bands, a handful of prolific local authors, and some of Spartanburg's biggest personalities, shoehorned them into the shell of a defunct eastside grocery store, then packed it for two nights with a huge community audience: *Hub City's Greatest Hits* at the "Historic Harris-Teeter Theater."

As Hub City's brand new (and new to town) programming director, part of my job was to put this show together—to make it seamless, funny, memorable. My theatre background was supposed to help. But with Hub City friends like Meg Barnhouse, Baker Maultsby, and Ashley Fly ready to add their Spartanburg flair to the mix, most of my job was done—content-wise, at least. The rest was all logistics.

But the logistics of turning an empty grocery store into a performance venue fit for this epic celebration were massive. Betsy and I must have written a hundred emails and made just as many phone calls arranging volunteers, security, circuit breakers, stage set-up, chair rental, floor cleaner, lighted exit signs, and kegs. I remember the kegs being of utmost importance.

Thinking back on it now though, fifteen years later, it wasn't the kegs or the logistics that were important to me those nights. What was important was how, for this non-native Spartanburger (and likely others in attendance), these shows were not only fun and funny nights, they also made this city feel like home for the first time—quirky, creative, and on the brink of something big. And how, while Hub City's Greatest Hits aimed to commemorate the past decade of their successes, it also seemed to announce a new beginning—a new chapter for both the Writers Project and the city that inspired it.

Facing page, from left: Peter Cooper, Fayssoux McLean, Baker Maultsby; Butler Brewton; Pat Jobe

"I find stories everywhere, in everything I read, in every conversation, in silent encounters during the course of every day."

THE STORYTELLER
Kirk H. Neely

During the tough years of the Great Recession, strong sales of three books by Spartanburg's beloved pastor kept Hub City Press alive and publishing.

I saw television for the first time when I was nine years old, and I was disappointed. Watching a flickering black-and-white screen was not nearly as entertaining as the stories that whetted my imagination when my grandfather spun a yarn. Storytelling is a treasured part of my heritage.

Stories are the vessels in which wisdom is contained. Aesop told fables, Biblical prophets told stories, Jesus told parables, and the best teachers have followed their examples. Stories are the containers into which moral instruction, deep pathos, and real humor are poured. I am sometimes asked, "Where do you get all of your stories?" For me, it is a matter of paying attention. I find stories everywhere, in everything I read, in every conversation, in silent encounters during the course of every day.

All stories tell the truth, even those that are fiction. In fact, fiction is one of the best ways to tell the truth. Storytelling, like story writing, rings true when it is about what you know and where you live. My stories are about my neck of the woods. Just like my blue jeans after an adventure in Dead Horse Canyon, my tales are caked with red clay. They are from the Blue Ridge Mountains, from the rivers of the Piedmont, from the cotton mills, and from the lumberyard.

My stories are about the ordinary—casseroles and sweet tea, black bears and beagle dogs, Tabasco sauce and fatback. My favorite stories are rooted and grounded in the South. Some will make you laugh out loud; others will bring a tear to your eye. All are memorable. I am grateful that Hub City Writers Project gave me the opportunity to write my stories. Some comfort like soul food. Others are as refreshing as a tall glass of iced tea. A few are spicy like shrimp and grits. My hope is that they will inspire you to tell a story or two about where you live and the people you know.

Southern Culture on the Skids
at HUB-BUB's Showroom

THE HUB-BUB IMPACT
Brad Steinecke

I was twenty-two years old in the summer of 2005, and after spending most of my life on a long and tedious trail of schooling, my future had opened onto a wilderness without any clear path. My half-baked plan to stay in New Orleans after graduation had fallen apart, and so I came home to Spartanburg, to my childhood bedroom at my parents' house, not exactly defeated but not with intention either. I'd keep my eyes open for opportunities and see what the world had to offer. Place didn't matter so much. A strong breeze could have led me nearly anywhere.

But to my surprise, the emerging community I discovered growing here around a new initiative called HUB-BUB reaffirmed and reinvigorated my Spartanburg roots. That community defied so many of my stale expectations about Spartanburg and connected me to people, stories, and potential that I'd never grasped in my earlier days here. It was refreshing and empowering, and it made me cheer for Spartanburg like I never had before.

Stickers announced the new website.

The city and others had finally recognized that Spartanburg had been losing generations of its talented young folks, not only to opportunities elsewhere, but to the belief that Spartanburg wasn't worth their effort. HUB-BUB confronted that with a thriving and newsy online message board, a bursting calendar of quirky events, and a commonality of purpose in celebrating Spartanburg's artfully weird side. Those days were a watershed moment for downtown, which then began to transform into the thriving place it is now. They were also foundational for me, in that I found a career tied to local culture, began fixing up a special old house, grew my family, and found fulfillment improving the little corner of the world I know best. It was a path I hadn't planned to take, but one that continues to define me and my place in Spartanburg.

HUB-BUB hosted more than six hundred public events in its nine-year run at The Showroom: concerts, art shows, plays, readings, films, and eclectic gatherings.

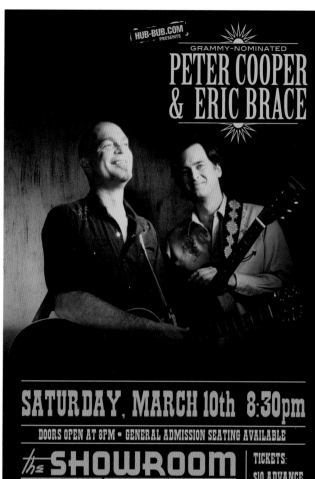
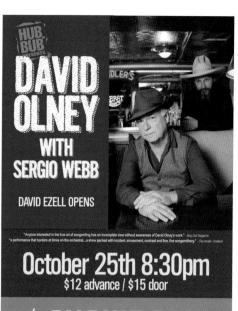

SHANE PRUITT BAND LIVE

Be in the audience for this special hometown show, being recorded for a live Shane Pruitt Band release.

FRIDAY, FEBRUARY 24th

9pm DOORS at 8:30   **$10/$12** ADVANCE /DOOR

The SHOWROOM
GALLERY & PERFORMANCE HALL
149 S. Daniel Morgan Ave. • Downtown Spartanburg

THE SHOWROOM hosted concerts almost every week, and each one of those shows got a carefully-crafted poster designed by HUB-BUB's Stephen Long. Taken as a whole, his catalog of music posters—and art, film, and community event posters— was perhaps the biggest, longest-running art project to come out of the HUB-BUB experiment. Stephen, who has a special love for mid-century modern design, made sure each poster was distinctive before they were placed on storefronts all over town. Lots of posters went home with the bands as mementos of special nights in downtown Spartanburg.

L to R: Jameelah Lang, Esteban del Valle, Greg Bae, Claudia Dishon

HUB-BUB ARTISTS IN RESIDENCE
Jameelah Lang

During its seven-year run at the building on South Daniel Morgan Avenue, the HUB-BUB Artist-in-Residence program brought thirty-three young writers and artists to Spartanburg for nine months of community creativity.

In 2009, I packed a trailer and drove for three days to an old brick building in South Carolina. I was twenty-one and had never left my Kansas hometown. In Spartanburg, I was given an apartment with high ceilings and pale blue walls. I shared the top floor with three other artists, each with their own brightly colored apartment. We were given a year to "live free and create."

What came of that year was my first publication. I wrote a story collection and received an MFA. I was accepted to a PhD program that led me to my first tenure-track job. Those are the facts, but they are not the truth.

Not the whole truth, at least, because what HUB-BUB gave me was much more vital and far more life-changing than any professional accomplishment. A year before Betsy called to invite me to HUB-BUB, I had ended a relationship with a violent man. I had stopped writing. I could no longer recognize myself, much less dream the shape my life might take. In the year before Spartanburg, I took a few cautious steps toward the person I imagined I could be.

Here is the whole truth: at HUB-BUB, I found a family that took me in without condition. Together, we slid down the age-worn rocks at old mills, ate tomato pie, and walked through snow drifts before dawn. My bedroom windows let in the sound of trains passing, without which I later found I couldn't sleep. I became engaged to a wonderful man, and together we had two sons who have broken me apart in a thousand beautiful ways. I became at HUB-BUB the person I am now: relentless, imperfect, loved.

I cannot pin down the moment the shift in me occurred. I can only say that there was magic at HUB-BUB: in that group of people, that brick building, that moment in time. There is magic in the city of Spartanburg, which from the sky looks like the hub in a wheel. The wheel's spokes are train tracks, and the city pulls each train to its center, sometimes holding them there for a while before they depart again.

EXPECTING GOODNESS
Kari Jackson Mailloux

I'm sure the question "But would this work in Spartanburg?" has been asked hundreds of times. The good thing is the answer is usually "Let's try it anyway."

That's how the Expecting Goodness Short Film Festival came to be from 2012 to 2014. Local emerging filmmaker Josh Foster adapted a short story into a short film, which gave him the idea to start a film festival with that premise. Josh eventually got connected to Stephen Long at HUB-BUB and me at the Hub City Writers Project. We decided our festival should focus on the Hub City Press book Expecting Goodness, a collection of stories by writers whose hometown is Spartanburg, edited by C. Michael Curtis.

The Expecting Goodness Short Film Festival celebrated the literature and film of South Carolina, providing opportunities for building a community between writers, filmmakers, and specialists across the film industry. Over several weeks, the project hosted community gatherings, workshops, lectures, and the concluding film festival during which the completed films were screened and awarded cash prizes. Winners also received a special HUB-BUB statuette: the Golden Bub. Seven filmmakers signed up to select a story from the collection and, over two months, created a short film inspired by that story to premiere on March 24, 2012 at the Showroom. That night, we charged five dollars at the door because we didn't know who would show up. But, in fact, it sold out, and we had to turn people away.

The following two years of the festival were even bigger, attracting dozens of recently published or award-winning short stories and filmmakers from across the state to premiere at the Chapman Cultural Center, as well as well-known judges from the film and writing industry with ties to Spartanburg.

We wanted Spartanburg to be known as a center of creative innovation and connection, and the response we received from writers, filmmakers, and the community proved that just about anything is possible in the Hub City.

When Hub City Assistant Director Kari Jackson moved home to Hutchison, Kansas, it marked the end of momentum for this amazing community project. We miss the festival but we miss Kari even more.

Facing page: festival awards ceremony. Below: a Golden Bub

For Here or To Go?
SPARTANBURG'S DRIVE-INS, DRIVE-THRUS, AND DINERS

BRANDY LEE LINDSEY and BAKER MAULTSBY
Photography by Carroll Foster and Jeffrey Young

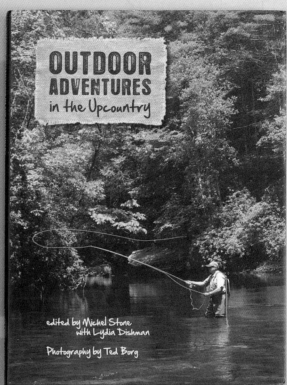

OUTDOOR ADVENTURES
in the Upcountry

edited by Michel Stone
with Lydia Dishman

Photography by Ted Borg

A TASTE OF
SPARTANBURG
LOCAL CHEFS · LOCAL FARMERS · LOCAL RECIPES

Ian Curcio,
Photographer

Ana Parra &
Amanda Richardson

Foreword by John T. Edge

BRANDY'S WORK

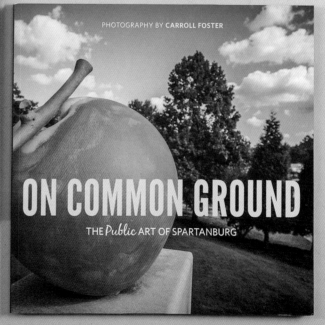

PHOTOGRAPHY BY CARROLL FOSTER

ON COMMON GROUND
THE *Public* ART OF SPARTANBURG

EMILY'S WORK

IN 2006, TEN YEARS AFTER OUR FIRST PUBLICATION, along came the multitalented poet Emily Louise Smith. She was not only our first writer-in-residence, she was a book designer! Truth be told, stalwart graphic artist Mark Olencki was ready for some assistance after designing thirty Hub City covers and interiors, and we were ready to pick up the pace. The next eight-year period saw nine different cover designers creating books on contract for Hub City, but the heaviest lifting was done by Emily (*The Whiskey Baron, Waking, Ask Mr. Smartypants, My Only Sunshine* etc.) and another new member of the Hub City family, Brandy Lindsey. They became our "Designing Women." Brandy got her start designing a book she edited, *For Here or To Go?: Spartanburg's Drive-Ins, Drive-Thrus, and Diners.* We loved her work so much we handed her all the photo/graphics-heavy color books: *On Common Ground: The Public Art of Spartanburg; Wild South Carolina: A Field Guild to Parks, Preserves and Special Places; A Taste of Spartanburg: Local Chefs, Local Farmers, Local Recipes* etc. With the hiring of Meg Reid in 2013 and Kate McMullen in 2017, we took most of our book design in-house, but this book you hold in your hands? That's Brandy Lindsey.

The Spartanburg Music Trail, launched by the Hub City Writers Project in 2011, honors twenty homegrown musicians who have made a national or international impact in the world of music. The Spartanburg Philharmonic now runs this project.

MARSHALL CHAPMAN

1949-

Marshall Chapman has been called Nashville's original female rock & roller. The daughter of a Spartanburg cotton mill owner, she has recorded more than a dozen albums, and her songs have been recorded by Emmylou Harris, Sawyer Brown (the top 5 country hit "Betty's Bein' Bad"), Joe Cocker, Jimmy Buffett, Irma Thomas and others. Her *Jaded Virgin* album was voted Record of the Year (1978) by *Stereo Review*. She continues recording and performing to this day.

THE SPARTANBURG MUSIC TRAIL
Marshall Chapman

(Wednesday, June 5, 2013)

I just remember how hot it was that day.

In that parking lot on East Saint John Street. I remember the mayor was there. My mother was there. My sister Dorothy … Joe Bennett of the Sparkletones was there. (The Sparkletones were also being honored.) The ubiquitous Chip Smith. Kimberly Childress Ward, daughter of Howard "Sparky" Childress (also of the Sparkletones) was there. Local musicians like Justin McCorkle and Matthew Knights. Plus a lot of people I didn't know—some of them fans of my music.

I was being honored by my hometown. It should've been one of the happiest days of my life. And in some ways it was. But lurking just below the surface, something wasn't right.

And the first person to notice was my sister, Dorothy. As soon as she saw my beloved husband Chris hobbling across the hot asphalt, she burst into tears.

Chris was in the throes of a drug relapse, but I was oblivious. I was too focused on my new album, *Blaze of Glory*, which had just been released the week before. It was fast coming out of the chute. Faster than any of my other albums. NPR was all over it. Americana Radio stations and Sirius XM radio were playing it like crazy. Starbucks had it on their in-store playlists worldwide. Plus it was getting rave reviews. Blurbs by Scotty Moore, Lucinda Williams, and Rodney Crowell. Artistically, I was on a roll. But personally, something was rotten in the state of Denmark.

It's hard to explain to my friends in Spartanburg the intensity involved in releasing a new album. Like any campaign, there is no limit to the amount of time, money and energy to be spent. For my sisters and female cousins, I liken it to putting on a wedding.

"Imagine putting on a wedding every night for three months, only you have to be in a different city every night, and you never get to sleep in your own bed." Their eyes always widen at this analogy. Oh my God, I had no idea!

The older I get, the more I realize the enormity of my hometown's musical legacy. And even with the Music Trail and Peter Cooper's wonderful book, *Hub City Music Makers*, I imagine a lot of people in Spartanburg still have no idea how far-reaching Spartanburg's musical legacy is.

Just today, I was in a Nashville studio. The recording session came to a halt when the studio's owner/engineer learned I was from Spartanburg. "Oh my God," he exclaimed. "Ira Tucker is the greatest singer who ever lived! That is so cool you're from there." I'd heard the Dixie Hummingbirds' music growing up, but had no idea they were from Spartanburg until I read Peter's book.

As for the Music Trail, I imagine it'll keep rolling along, just like life itself. And speaking of life, mine descended into darkness there for a while. Chris and I divorced a year and a half after that hot afternoon in the parking lot on East Saint John Street. Then, the day after our divorce was final, my formidable mother died. A week after that, I was quarantined at Saint Thomas Hospital in Nashville with something called C.diff Colitis that damn near killed me. But enough of that. Fast forward four years. Miraculously, one day at a time, Chris and I are seeing each other again. And we both seem to be doing better than ever. Which has a lot of people (myself included) scratching their heads. Because it makes no more sense than Ira Tucker emerging from the Jim Crow South to become the greatest singer who ever lived.

THE ARRIVAL OF MIKE CURTIS
Betsy Teter

When I first heard that legendary fiction editor C. Michael Curtis was moving to Spartanburg back in 2006, I remember wondering if he would walk among mortals like us. Curtis had been selecting short stories for *The Atlantic* magazine for more than forty years, and now he was coming to the home of the Hub City Writers Project. Curtis was one of American literature's great fiction editors—a man who was among the first to publish Ann Beattie, Louise Erdrich, John Sayles, Bobbie Ann Mason, among others.

Curtis and his wife, novelist and poet Elizabeth "Betsy" Cox, were leaving Boston for jobs at Wofford College. *The Atlantic* was cutting costs and Curtis could now do his job from afar. Hub City had completed its first decade, and we dreamed of breaking out as a literary publisher. One day, John Lane came home from a Wofford English Department meeting and said Curtis was looking for ways to be more involved in the local writing community. "Let's put him on the editorial board," he said. So in 2007, one of the greatest fiction editors in America joined ten local writers around a folding table at the Hub City offices as we sorted through what books we would publish next. I remember him grousing, "You need to publish books that look more like New York books." To keep him engaged, I suggested he edit a collection of short stories that would be "the essential fiction of Spartanburg."

We began feeding Mike novel submissions to read. Most he rejected, but with his help, we inched toward becoming a publisher known for solid literary fiction. He provided important literary advice and reached out to friends like Lauren Groff, Elizabeth Berg, and ZZ Packer to judge our contests or keynote our conferences. He edited novel submissions by Michel Stone, Susan Tekulve, Julia Franks, Thomas McConnell, and others. "Mike went through my whole novel—all 387 typescript pages—three times," McConnell says. "After an editing feat like that, I know this: give him a sharp pencil and a line to hone and he's a happy man."

Suffice it to say, with Mike Curtis on board, we are all happy people.

Hub City's C. Michael Curtis prize is awarded to an exemplary manuscript from a Southern writer.

"After more than forty years living in Boston and working for *The Atlantic* and *The Atlantic Monthly Press*, I was pleased to discover the Hub City Writers Project, and even more pleased to become involved in its determination to find, and publish, the written work of local and regional authors. Spartanburg is richer for the good fortune that nurtured Hub City."

MINNOW
James E. McTeer II
"A visionary novel of a world gone mad."
—MICHAEL FARRIS SMITH
EMBER
A NOVEL
BROCK ADAMS
SCOTT SHARPE
A Wild Eden
WINNER of the SOUTH CAROLINA NOVEL PRIZE
MINNOW James E. McTeer II
EMBER BROCK ADAMS
A Wild Eden SHARPE
In the Garden of Stone SUSAN TEKULVE
Mercy Creek Matt Matthews
Brian Ray Through the Pale Door
FICTION

THE SOUTH CAROLINA NOVEL PRIZE
Susan Tekulve

In the early summer of 2012, I received a conference call from Betsy Teter and Sara June Goldstein of the Arts Commission, announcing I'd won the South Carolina First Novel Prize. I could hear happiness in their voices as they delivered the news. Hub City Press would publish my novel, *In the Garden of Stone*. Then, Betsy said, "By the way, Mike Curtis likes your book. He wants to be your directing editor. He'll be in touch."

This illustrious fiction editor of *The Atlantic* volunteered as an editor for Hub City Press, and had read my novel—twice, it turned out. I met Mike at the Deli Corner, a German restaurant in Spartanburg, where Mike gave me a print copy of my 360-page manuscript, its pages fluttering with neon pink Post-It notes. Before we jumped into the line edits, we ate pastrami sandwiches, and talked. Mike told me he liked the pioneer spirit of the novel, and the way the characters endured. I mentioned that my book, which is set in Depression-era Southwest Virginia, and follows the lives of a Sicilian immigrant family living in coal and railroad country, was a work of endurance. I spent eight years writing this multi-generational family tale, and another two years revising it.

I realize now that Mike started the publication process by creating a comfort level that would allow him to say all the constructive things editors, and publishers, need to say in order to usher a writer's book into the world. Following that, the Hub City staff involved me with all parts of the production process—the cover design, the galleys, the marketing plan. In the spring of 2013, the press hosted a launch for the book, and guests came from Spartanburg, Greenville, Clemson. Someone from Southwest Virginia arrived, bearing a bouquet of orange day lilies she picked from her garden because, she noticed, these flowers figure into passages throughout the book. This gesture remains burned in my memory, the flowers emblematic of my experience with Hub City Press, whose staff members are attentive to detail, steadfast, so quietly professional that you don't notice, until you notice, how graceful and enduring they are.

Susan was the third winner of the South Carolina First Novel Prize (now the South Carolina Novel Prize), which is biennially co-sponsored by the Hub City Writers Project, South Carolina Arts Commission, South Carolina Humanities, and the State Library. Other winners have come from Greenville, Spartanburg, Easley, and Columbia. Judges have included Ben Fountain, Percival Everett, Bret Lott, Josephine Humphreys, Bridgett Davis, Jill McCorkle, and Stephanie Powell Watts.

THE IGUANA TREE
Michel Stone

The Iguana Tree began with a writing prompt during a workshop at Hub City's 2004 Writing in Place conference. That little paragraph describing a Mexican girl in a rocking chair later became a short story that won Hub City's annual fiction contest, which sent me to Wildacres Writers Workshop in North Carolina for a week. Encouraged by Ron Rash, Gail Galloway Adams, and others I met there, I decided to expand my story into a novel— the story of a Texas border crossing—which Hub City published in 2012.

When favorable reviews began rolling in, I was blown away. I was invited to give readings all across the country: at literary festivals, book clubs, at an immigration conference in Texas (I asked the director if he realized I just made stuff up; he said yes). Four colleges selected the novel as Freshman Read, a town in Oregon used the book for a community read, Clemson University invited me to be their convocation speaker in front of an audience of thirty-five hundred, and Converse College had me as their commencement speaker. In summer 2014 I was even asked to be the keynote at Hub City's summer workshop where my journey had begun years earlier.

While I was speaking to that crowd in Hermiston, Oregon, an attendee suggested I write a follow-up novel, and when I tentatively agreed (a bluff), the room exploded into applause. Then I had little choice. I completed my second novel, *Border Child*, fourteen months later and signed with literary agent Marly Rusoff. She sold the manuscript to legendary Random House editor Nan Talese, and I was off on book tour again! That one writing prompt sparked a journey of experiences, lessons, and friendships I'd never imagined, and it gave me the confidence, finally, to call myself a writer.

The Iguana Tree is Hub City's best-selling book of all time.

THE HUB CITY WRITERS PROJECT
INVITES YOU TO A SPECIAL
BOOK RELEASE EVENT FOR

MICHEL STONE
AUTHOR OF
THE IGUANA TREE
7-9 PM
MONDAY, MARCH 12
THE SHOWROOM
149 S. DANIEL MORGAN AVE.

REGRETS: INFO@HUBCITY.ORG

CAN'T COME? PURCHASE BOOK AT WWW.HUBCITY.ORG/PRESS

BUILDING A BOOKSTORE
Betsy Teter

The idea for the Hub City Bookshop woke me in the middle of the night. In the darkness of my bedroom I remember thinking, "That's it. That's the answer."

It was the fall of 2009, twelve months into the Great Recession, and the Writers Project was beginning to founder. Pic-A-Book, Hub City's number-one customer, had closed its doors. The company that distributed Hub City books to the chain stores had collapsed, owing us thousands of dollars. My assistant had quit after I cut her hours so drastically she couldn't make ends meet. For the first time, we were postponing publication of books in hopes we'd have enough money next year.

It was a crazy idea: ramping up, opening a bookstore while the future looked so dark. The next day, I stopped to peer into the empty storefront of the Masonic Temple, just up the street from our office at HUB-BUB. *Hmmm*, I thought. *Why not try a Hail Mary pass*?

I scheduled a lunch with outgoing Mayor Bill Barnet, who had always wanted a bookstore downtown and was moving his residence two doors down from the Temple. Could we bring a coffee shop, he asked? Of course, I said, then begged Little River Roasting and Cakehead Bakery to come on board. The winning ticket came when Bill told the folks planning his mayoral departure shindig to cancel the party and instead have everyone make donations towards our bookstore. Ten weeks later, with $300,000 in gifts and pledges, construction was underway. We spun off HUB-BUB and went full-throttle into the book business.

And now ten years later, we have a thriving literary organization that has spawned similar non-profit bookstores all over the country, including ones in Milwaukee, Winston-Salem, Tulsa, Chicago, and elsewhere. Hub City Bookshop has been twice named as among *Southern Living*'s Best in the South, and in 2019, authors attending the annual convention of Southern Independent Booksellers Association awarded us the Bibb's Pick, recognizing us as a bookstore that is "warm, welcoming, inclusive and knowledgeable, always with a smile."

WEDDING PULLS

poems

J.K. DANIELS

THE NEW SOUTHERN VOICES PRIZE
Eric Kocher

I moved to Spartanburg in 2011 to spend a year as a writer-in-residence for the Hub City Writers Project. At the end of that year, I wasn't quite ready to leave, mostly because Betsy and I had been talking about starting a book prize for a poetry collection and it seemed like we might be able to pull it off. A few months later we had a logo designed by former HUB-BUB artist-in-residence Mark Rice and, somehow, had National Book Critics Circle Award winning poet, D.A. Powell, signed on as a judge. We've now had four winners of the New Southern Voices Poetry Prize and four astonishing collections of poetry have made their way into the world. Each one has taught us something new—or reminded us of something necessary and familiar—about what it means to be alive here and now in this small corner of the world. As of June 2020, my decision to stick around for a few months and see this prize through will have been extended by nine years, which makes each of these books, for me, sing a little bit louder and more clearly about the place I've come to think of as my home.

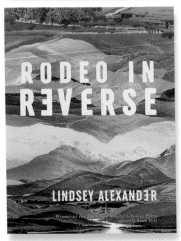

HUB CITY
farmers market
MORE THAN JUST A MARKET

HUB CITY SCOOPS

HUB CITY DELIVERY

HUB CITY CHURCH

186

HUB CITY BOOKSHOP

HUB CITY PRESS

HUB CITY WRITERS PROJECT

THE HUB OF THE HUBS
Betsy Teter

This article appeared in the Herald-Journal in 2015 for Hub City's 20th anniversary.

There are a few other Hub Cities in America, but certainly none more enthusiastic about the nickname than Spartanburg, where there has been a veritable explosion of local institutions adopting that moniker. And from where we sit in the offices of the Hub City Writers Project, well, we Spartanburg writers just might have had something to do with that.

All this hub talk in Spartanburg appears to have started way back in the 1880s, when local boosters looked at all the railroad tracks coming through town and made this observation: "A glimpse at the map will show the city of Spartanburg to resemble the hub of a great wheel with spokes running in five directions."

By the turn of the 20th century, if you were traveling by rail, Spartanburg was on the way to just about everywhere. In order to get their textile goods to market, Spartanburg's industrialists went on a frenzy of track-building. And in 1925 along came Hayne Shop, a gigantic Southern Railway train car repair facility, bringing hundreds of high-paying jobs. A light bulb went on in the heads of the men at the Chamber of Commerce: *Hey, Spartanburg is the Hub City of the Piedmont!*

Thus ensued the first Hub City wave in Spartanburg. In 1926 Hub City Ice Cream opened, followed closely by Hub City Lumber Co., Electric Co., Barbershop, and Candy Store. By 1930 there was a newspaper called the Hub City Observer, a diner called Hub City Lunch, and Hub City Garage. In 1938 somebody opened The Hub department store, a Radio Service, and a Feed and Building Supply.

The 1940s brought Hub City Oil Co., Hub City Courts public housing, Hub City Auto Sales and—my favorite—Hubba Hubba Ice Cream. And then the Hub City craze was over as quickly as it began. A lone Hub City Finance company was established in the 1960s, as Spartanburg moved on to more sparkly nicknames: The Crossroads of the New South, and, yes, Sparkle City.

The Hub City era was over ... until a little group of writers gathered in a coffee shop on Morgan Square in the mid-'90s and decided to resurrect this name. It was how we would stake our claim to a new Spartanburg—culturally creative, progressive, and a beacon for writers and artists.

It started slowly. The Hub City Writers Project, after all, had no office and was releasing just one book a year (most with Hub City in the title). But the meme was working itself into the community consciousness. A Hub City Bakery emerged in 2002, followed by Hub City Coffee and Hub City Grille. The Hub City Co-op Grocery was organized. A farmers market, a church, a railroad museum all adopted the name. There was Hub City Hog Fest, the Hub City Connector rail trail, Hub City Empty Bowls charity project, and a hot dog shop named Hub Diggity. Our own Hub City Bookshop opened in 2010. Soon thereafter: Hub City Delivery, Hub City Scoops, Hub City Brewfest, Hub City Pharmacy.

So with this crazy flurry of Hub City activity, we writers have something to say to all the other Hub Cities—from Lubbock, TX to Hattiesburg, MS, from Crestview, FL to Albany, OR , from Lafayette, LA and Aberdeen, SD to Marshfield, WI, Oelwein, IA and Elizabethtown, KY. Give it up. You are beaten. A Google search of business names will confirm: Spartanburg is the undisputed Hub City champion. We are the Hub of the Hubs. Write it down.

WRITERS SPEAKING OUT LOUD

Meg Reid

In April 2014 my mother and grandmother were in town on one of their first visits since I had taken a job at Hub City Press. On a warm Friday afternoon, we met Betsy and John at the wine bar next to the bookshop. What was supposed to be a quick drink before Jazz on the Square quickly turned into a scheming session. The state Legislature had just slashed the budgets of two universities because they selected LGBT books for freshman reading programs. One of the books in question was Hub City's own *Out Loud: The Best of Rainbow Radio*, a collection of radio essays edited by Ed Madden and Candace Chellew-Hodge, assigned to students at USC Upstate. The Legislature's action made national news, and we were receiving notes of outrage from writers across the nation.

We knew we had to do something to make clear these legislators didn't speak for us. We decided on t-shirts emblazoned with: "I'm speaking out! Support academic freedom. Fight government censorship!" Wouldn't it be great if a couple of writers sent in photos wearing the shirt with testimonials supporting the campaign? Betsy and I worked through the weekend. Emails went out, asking: "Do you want to join us and stand up for academic freedom?" Authors wrote back and forwarded the message on to others. Stephen Long quickly mocked up a design. A week later, our offices were strewn with the colorful neon shirts and stacks and stacks of priority envelopes.

Our lives became consumed by cold-emailing, shipping shirts, and posting daily photos to social media. By the end of the month, our campaign had garnered support from John Green, Junot Díaz, Ann Patchett, Emma Donoghue, Richard Ford, Terrance Hayes, Pat Conroy, and dozens of others. It accrued thousands of followers across social media platforms and was covered in *Publishers Weekly* and *The Guardian* newspaper in the UK. In early May, the state Senate voted to restore the funding but said the colleges must spend a comparable amount of money on teaching the Constitution, the Declaration of Independence, and the Federalist Papers (something the schools were, undoubtedly, already doing). While the Legislature's final decision was, in the end, a qualified victory, the Out Loud campaign was not. It was a beautiful moment where we stood up for our beliefs, our books, and the fascinating and challenging ways literature changes our world for the better.

Below: Junot Diaz. Facing page, clockwise from top left: Percival Everett, Robert Bausch, Kwame Dawes, John Green, Terrance Hayes, Masha Hamilton

FROM THE BEGINNING, Hub City has been a partnership with artists. We invited Southern Exposure, a local artists' collective, to present work in *Hub City Anthology*, and again in its sequel. As part of the Lawson's Fork project, we commissioned Berry Bate, a Converse College graduate, to create a towering magnolia sculpture in Glendale to celebrate the rebirth of the creek. A year later, as *Textile Town* was released, we asked memorabilia artist Ellen Kochansky to weave together two hundred items donated by seventy-five locals into a giant "Mill Memories" piece that hangs at the Chapman Cultural Center. Our books, *Artists Among Us* (2011) and *On Common Ground* (2015), spotlight the work of scores of Spartanburg artists. We regularly publish the work of the best local photographers, including Clay Bolt, who captured this fox for *Web of Water*, then went on to shoot for *National Geographic*. And to make sure we keep our eyes on our mission, Dorothy Josey's portraits of Flannery O'Connor and Eudora Welty watch over us at our offices.

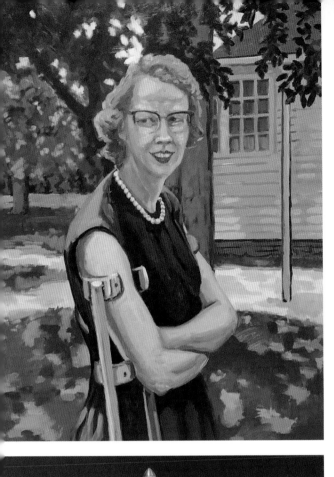

WRITING IN PLACE
Bobbie Jean Shepard

Writing in Place, Hub City's longest-running program, has been held on the campus of Wofford College for the past twenty-one years.

When I first attended Hub City's writers conference nearly fifteen years ago, I was a young mother and teacher who needed a retreat, a weekend to gather ideas for the classroom and regain my creative identity. I had written a few poems in college but felt insecure about my abilities beyond teaching high school English. I have always loved poetry but could not call myself a poet.

I've attended at least six summers, maybe more. I return because the workshops offer variety and growth. I have gained experience under the guidance of many poets—some who write lengthy, esoteric poems, some who compose shorter, abstract works, and others whose allusions range from comic book heroes to the rural South. Among these are Kate Daniels, Gary Jackson, Emily Rosko, and Ray McManus. Each has brought a unique voice to instruction. Each exercise—whether listening to music or illustrating a scene—has challenged me to see myself as a writer and made me feel more comfortable composing. Sure, I still get nervous when we share on Saturday—what pressure to share after writing so quickly! But every year I am amazed at what my peers craft under the guidance of these gifted writers, and I feel myself growing more confident in the creative process. This community encourages me to keep writing, to work toward deadlines (real or imagined), and to submit for publication.

Last year I invited a friend to join me. He, too, sees himself more as an English teacher than a creative writer and felt uncertain about writing and sharing drafts with others, especially the accomplished writers. And yet, as the weekend unfolded, he expressed the same pleasure and surprise I have experienced each year: meeting people who cherish the written word, time to wrestle with ideas that you have carried for years, the gentle encouragement of strangers who become friends, and the inspiration that you leave with—a desire to return to the page.

THE BOOKSELLER
Anne Waters

I began selling books at a downtown independent bookstore shortly after college in my hometown, Little Rock, where we counted Bill and Hillary Clinton among our regular customers. When Capitol Bookstore closed, I moved on to independent publishing where I would spend the majority of my career. Moving to Spartanburg in 2013 and joining the Hub City Writers Project to manage our not-for-profit bookshop truly brought my career full circle.

When Jeff Bezos launched Amazon, he did so at the American Booksellers Association's annual BookExpo in Chicago in 1995. I was one of only a couple of dozen publishing professionals curious enough to show up at his early morning informational breakfast meeting. In exchange, I received a voucher to order a free book from their trade show booth. As promised, the book I ordered awaited me when I returned home. I was both impressed and terrified.

It may seem a miracle that small independent bookstores survive and even thrive today, but according to Harvard researcher Ryan Raffaelli there are three reasons why. We provide "Community, Curation, and Convening." Independent bookstores, or "indies," were early champions of the "buy local" movement. Unlike big-box stores where buying choices are made far from the communities they serve, indie book buyers are careful with curation of books we stock. At the Hub City Bookshop we are looking for hidden gems: unique small-budget books, fresh and diverse voices, and books that are carefully edited and designed. Just like the ones published by Hub City Press.

Indie bookstores provide a place for people to meet and share ideas. To that end, our store offers more than one hundred readings annually, most of which are free and open to the public. We even have been the site of one wedding and at least one marriage proposal. Most importantly, we are driven by our customers. If you google "handselling," you will find it defined as "the practice of promoting books by personal recommendation rather than by publisher-sponsored marketing." I think it's worth noting that this practice refers to the promotion of *books*.

Ten years ago, Hub City Bookshop opened its doors to provide a place where we could sell our growing list of publications and to serve as an anchor for our community. Thank you, Spartanburg, for supporting us for the first ten years. We look forward to the next ten.

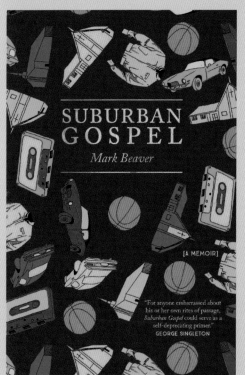

SUBURBAN GOSPEL
Mark Beaver

[A MEMOIR]

"For anyone embarrassed about his or her own rites of passage, *Suburban Gospel* could serve as a self-deprecating primer."
GEORGE SINGLETON

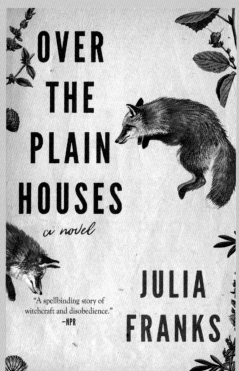

OVER THE PLAIN HOUSES

a novel

"A spellbinding story of witchcraft and disobedience."
–NPR

JULIA FRANKS

"*Watershed* will leave you charged and enlightened. Mark Barr is a powerhouse."
— SMITH HENDERSON, *author of Fourth of July Creek*

WATERSHED

A NOVEL

MARK BARR

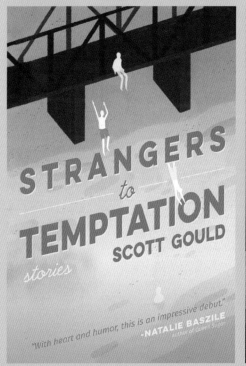

STRANGERS to TEMPTATION
SCOTT GOULD
stories

"With heart and humor, this is an impressive debut."
-NATALIE BASZILE
author of Queen Sugar

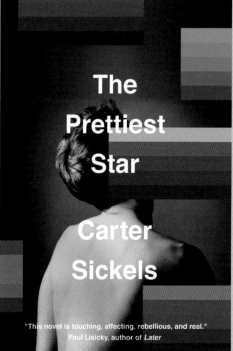

The Prettiest Star

Carter Sickels

"This novel is touching, affecting, rebellious, and real."
Paul Lisicky, author of *Later*

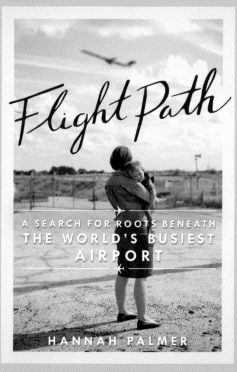

Flight Path

A SEARCH FOR ROOTS BENEATH THE WORLD'S BUSIEST AIRPORT

HANNAH PALMER

JUDGING A BOOK BY ITS COVER
Meg Reid

People often ask me what makes a great Hub City Press book cover. I tell them there isn't any key to a perfect cover. Though I will admit there are certain tendencies that make themselves obvious when you scan a recent catalog of ours. You'll see that I'm a fan of left-aligned text in the center and bottom half of a cover and I rarely put any elements at the top. I love yellows, greens, and blues. I like a cover that strikes a balance between familiar and surprising. I like neutral covers that don't immediately broadcast the gender of the author.

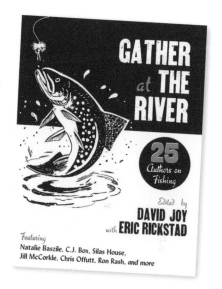

We publish a lot of debut writers here. A debut writer doesn't have an established brand, which means the options for a cover are limitless, but also the cover has to make an introduction to every person who sees it. Likewise, we publish work that's decidedly literary but sometimes has a commercial edge. There are certain commercial cover tropes that can be employed with a very light hand to a literary cover that make it more compelling and accessible to a larger audience. I find these tropes act as both constraints and opportunities for more creativity.

Whatever style has developed since I arrived in 2013 has happened incrementally over time. With each book I design, I more finely tune my sense of what is *right* for both that particular book and the press at large. I spend a lot of time thinking about whether the book is firmly placed enough in the real world to warrant a photograph. Or if—like many of our novels—it has a touch of the unreal that only an illustration can do justice. I spend time researching illustrators and watching trends. For this, the bookshop has been invaluable. Walking through the bookshop each day gives me ample opportunity to see and touch the work of other designers working in my medium. I believe our materials and finishes should match those of not only other independent presses but larger publishers as well.

The best part for me is that as we have grown and expanded both our reach and the range of our authors, I've felt free to take more risks on design. I can step further out of a comfortable space because I know our readers trust us, knowing a Hub City Press book will always be both beautifully written and thoughtfully packaged.

Meg has designed more than thirty covers for Hub City since 2013.

PHOTOGRAPHING CAROLINA WRITERS AT HOME
Rob McDonald

From Beaufort to Boone and a dozen places in between, Carolina Writers at Home, *published in 2015, showcases the houses where some of the most notable Southern authors forged their writing lives.*

Making the photographs for *Carolina Writers at Home* began with a long, hot drive from Virginia to Spartanburg in the summer of 2014 and ended with a blustery ferry ride from Hilton Head Island to Daufuskie that December. In between, I spent the near equivalent of two weeks eating free motel breakfasts, logging 4,012 miles in sixty-eight hours and fifty-two minutes—not counting episodes of sitting in stalled traffic—simply driving from one place to the next. The yield was seventy-seven rolls of film, containing 922 individual negatives, to be processed and scanned.

It was an intense effort involving some creative scheduling, but the beautiful finished book is unlike anything I have worked on in this double life I have lived for two decades as a photographer and teacher of literature and writing. I have always thought of myself as a photographer of place, but these are very personal, sometimes intimate, images. They display individuality, disposition, ways of being in the world. I sometimes wish I had kept a written diary of my responses. The familiarity of Holly Goddard Jones' home office piled high with baby equipment. The strangeness of Daniel Wallace's glass-eye collection. The overflowing ashtray next to George Singleton's laptop. The twinkling lights and whimsy of Jill McCorkle's upstairs writing space. The November light illuminating the little pair of grooms on Ed Madden's bookshelf. Kathryn Stripling Byer's woodland garden. Nikky Finney's National Book Award medal resting on a dark wood sideboard.

I am still astonished that any of the writers who contributed to this collection let a stranger with a camera poke around their lives without restriction or apparent inhibition. Their generosity, and Meg Reid's thoughtful placement of the photographs in context with the authors' essays—using them more for amplification than illustration—make this book glow.

Facing page, clockwise from top left: Nikky Finney, Ed Madden, J. Drew Lanham, Dot Jackson

PART OF HUB CITY'S MISSION is to ensure we are raising the next generation of writers and readers in our home community. From summer creative writing camps to teen open mics, Hub City continues to serve Spartanburg's young people. In the past eight years our Growing Great Readers program has given away more than twenty thousand new summer reading books to elementary school children in our city's disadvantaged neighborhoods. Since 2007, we have hosted the annual regional competition for Poetry Out Loud, a teen poetry recitation contest created by the National Endowment for the Arts. Our Books at the Bus Stop program provides free books to children and adults who use public transportation. In 2020 we started a bilingual reading series for children at the Franklin School, and we created the Books as Mirrors program, a homegrown initiative to stock local school libraries with thousands of diverse and culturally relevant children's books.

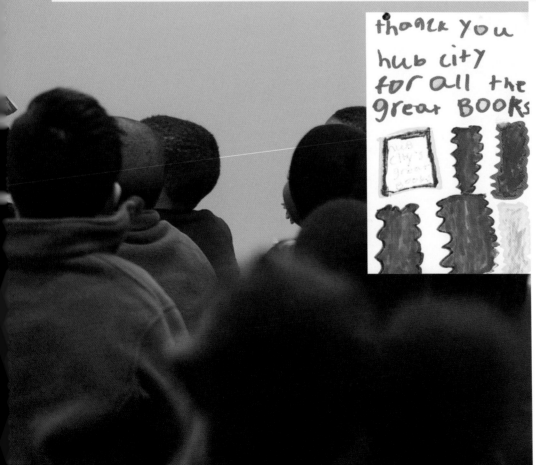

Left: Former Hub City Outreach Director Leslie Sainz at the Franklin School. Above: Thank you cards from students.

THE IPPY AWARDS
recognize the year's best independently published titles. So far we have twenty-two of them—gold, silver, and bronze. Twice, Hub City novels have been named the best in the world in this contest: *Over the Plain Houses* by Julia Franks (2016), and *Whiskey & Ribbons* by Leesa-Cross Smith (2018).

THE WILMINGTON CONNECTION
Emily Louise Smith

In my publishing classes at the University of North Carolina Wilmington, I often refer to Hub City as "the mothership." My year as the first writer-in-residence launched my publishing career, and the term feels apt for an organization currently powered by such a dynamic team of women. When I arrived in Spartanburg in 2006, co-founders Gary, John, and Betsy were daily fixtures and sources of wisdom in the new digs on Daniel Morgan, but it was Betsy's bustling desk around which people and projects seemed to constellate. I listened as she earned the trust of authors, finessed layouts, negotiated with vendors, packed houses, and convinced everyone in her path—including the eager pupil leaning ever closer—that books build community. By the time I left to direct UNCW's Publishing Laboratory a year later, her tireless advocacy had infused every fiber of my being.

Based on Hub City's model, I founded Lookout Books to champion debut and historically underrepresented voices. I also envisioned it as an apprenticeship in everything Betsy had taught me—close editing, imaginative promotion, beautiful design, community engagement. Twelve years later, I'm still working to create opportunities for my students to put the pieces together to start vital conversations around books. Hub City remains the gold standard in my classes, so it's little wonder that four UNCW alumni—director Meg Reid, assistant director Kate McMullen, former writer-in-residence Corinne Manning, and former press assistant Rachel Richardson—eventually found their way to the mothership.

When a clever media campaign catches my eye, I miss Kate's knack for combining design and story. Rachel reminds me how fun it can be to discover a book, and I have Corinne to thank for initiatives that continue to refine my thinking as a publisher. I don't know how I weathered my first years teaching and launching a press, but I do know that Meg's creativity, instinct for publishing, and friendship made my work then, as now, better.

Betsy, Meg, and Kate have worked together longer than I did with any of them. I feel only a tinge of jealousy. Mostly I feel inspired—as I watch them build new platforms for authors who are redefining perceptions of the American South in literature, when they "pubsplain" me or reveal a gorgeous cover, every time they return to my class to encourage the next generation of publishers, and remind me that I learned mentorship from the best.

Facing page, L to R: Meg Reid, Emily Louise Smith, Kate McMullen

THE
MAGNETIC
GIRL

UNABRIDGED

OF THE 2018 SOUTH CAROLINA NOVEL PRIZE

À
WILD
EDEN

SCOTT

UNABRIDGED

CONNELL

THE
WOODEN
KING

UNABRIDGED
READ BY STEFAN RUDNICKI

MINNO

Un roman
de JAMES E.
McTEER II

RENTRÉE
LITTÉRAIRE

"Minn
une vé
Ce livre
cou et e
avec un
digne d
Toni M

Éditions
du sous-
sol

PEOPLE ALL OVER THE PLANET are reading and listening to Hub City books. In 2014 Hub City Press kicked off a new era of foreign editions when we sold rights to *The Whiskey Baron* by Jon Sealy to the French publisher Les éditions Albin Michel. Other Hub City books have been translated into Czech, Korean, German, and Vietnamese. All recent Hub City novels are now published in audio form too, as we play our part in the rapidly expanding audiobook movement. And if you'd rather read our books on a device, most of the books we've published in the last ten years are available for download. These new formats strengthen our brand and build our reach, allowing our books to capture as many eyes (and ears!) as possible worldwide.

David Joy

Diane Chamberlain

THE HUB CITY BOOKSHOP hosts more than one hundred author events each year, from nationally-touring writers to self-published locals.

Victor LaValle

Kwame Alexander

Smith Henderson

REAL DADS STAND UP!

EVER WONDER HOW CATCH PHRASES ARE BORN? All it took for Hub City was some office brainstorming around three words: Read, Write, and South. We did what we do best and didn't overthink it. Broken down to basics, these three words are the core of our mission to cultivate readers and nurture writers in our home territory. We rolled out our slogan and design on t-shirts and totes for our first Book 'n' Brew celebration with Ron Rash in September 2018. Local photography phenom Zach Parks helped us take it viral. The merch continues to be popular, and you can find our fans sporting it from coast to coast.

SIBA COMES TO TOWN
Kate McMullen

Pulling up to trade shows with boxes of Hub City books to sling is always
a great feeling. San Antonio, Portland, Tampa, Atlanta—we've traveled the
whole country. But in September 2019 Meg and I loaded her car at the
Hub City Bookshop and drove the half-mile to the Spartanburg Marriott.
The Southern Independent Booksellers Alliance was bringing its annual
book show to our city. That meant five hundred booksellers, authors, and
publishing professionals were going to pack local hotels, fill up downtown
restaurants, and have the opportunity to see up close what we've built at the
Hub City Writers Project.

Back in grad school, one of my first gigs as a wee publisher was planning an
author tour at Lookout Books, which meant I could attend SIBA 2015 in Raleigh. This
was the weekend I first met Meg Reid, who hired me two years later as assistant director of Hub
City Press. SIBA is one of my favorite trade shows, partly because this first experience made me
feel *in*, finally part of the industry I had chosen to break into.

When we first heard SIBA had taken our bait to come to Spartanburg, naturally the first thing Meg
and I thought was: *let's throw a party.* Cue our fearless headlong leap into anything with custom cocktails
and mingling with folks who are readers and writers like us. Cue my pitch for the purchase of giant light-
up letters spelling H U B C I T Y and then ordering them off a website called tablecloths.com. Cue a big
order for brightly colored Read Write South t-shirts for staff and board members to wear.

Anne Waters booked us a beautiful-if-dusty unleased space in the newly renovated
Montgomery Building. It was loud. It had rained. One of the coolers sprang a leak. So many people
showed up that we threatened to run out of drinks, and the party spilled into the arcade and onto
a narrow sidewalk on bustling Church Street. It was Hub City at its finest. The next morning,
everyone was either thrilled they'd come or sorry they'd missed it. It felt like one of the gatherings
we'd talk about for another ten years.

Facing page, top: Kate McMullen, Carter Sickels, Meg Reid, and Mark Barr at the Hub City SIBA booth.
Left, Betsy Teter on the exhibition floor;. Right, hundreds of booksellers at the Marriott Spartanburg

Bookseller Kyla Burwick

COVID-19
Anne Waters

The pandemic officially arrived for the Hub City Writers Project on March 15, 2020, four hours before Delicious Reads, our annual writer-in-the-round fundraiser at the AC Hotel. That morning we hastily canceled the sold-out event, though a few determined ticket buyers trickled into the bookshop to meet a small number of shell-shocked authors. Within three days, we closed our doors to the public to protect both customers and staff, knowing that a shut-down order from the Governor was likely.

Behind those locked doors, staff moved into a creative high gear. To survive, we knew we had to connect with readers and writers with ingenuity, regularity, humor, and grace. We launched the Buy a Book in April campaign on the internet by directing followers to a brand-new online shopping portal, bookshop.org, which shared thirty percent of each sale with us. A month later we were proud to report that we had sold 571 books there. We delivered books at curbside and through the mail. We marketed gift cards and curated book bundles. In May, in time for Mother's Day, we initiated Books by Bicycle; writer-in-residence Aurora Masum-Javed brought books to happy customers' doorsteps via her shiny, red bicycle. In short, we hustled.

Covid-19 gave us the opportunity to go back to our roots: collecting the voices of our community, just as the Federal Writers Project did in the Great Depression. Leslie Sainz coordinated a new blog called "Sheltering in Spartanburg," which presented interviews and essays from homefolks trying to manage through the shutdown. Writing workshops went online through Zoom, as did book clubs and author events. Video became our most important tool. Each week staff members made book recommendations on social media, and our popular Pubsplaining videos with Meg Reid and Kate McMullen became Instagram Live Happy Hours. Hub City Press had to make quick decisions, too. The lead spring title, *The Prettiest Star*, was kept in the warehouse for a month to avoid releasing it when every bookstore in the country was shuttered. Meantime, we created a series of virtual events for author Carter Sickles—live videos with national authors such as Wiley Cash, Rebekka Makkai, and Paul Lisicky.

As Spartanburg slowly opened up in mid-May, so did we—cautiously—at twenty percent occupancy. Staff wore rubber gloves and bookshelf-fabric face coverings sewn by board member Latria Graham. We knew Covid would be with us for a while, but we'd learned how to navigate it.

THE ANNEX
Meg Reid

What's it like to create and renovate a new office during a global pandemic? In a word: chaotic. Of course, we didn't plan it that way when we first viewed the space at 200 Ezell in late January. We took in the reception area with its beautiful windows facing the back of the Hub City Bookshop, heard the train whistle from the nearby tracks. Even though the space—which we jokingly at first, and then more seriously, referred to as "The Annex"—was just a former law office with old ceramic tiles and frayed carpets, we saw through the cosmetic defects to its old building charm. The big windows and the loading dock served as a reminder of the building's early life as a warehouse for a wagon maker.

For a decade Hub City Press functioned out of the back of the bookshop—a congenial elbow-to-elbow setup that was great for collaboration but not so much for close-reading and editing. My workspace was a desk set against a concrete wall, as far from the glass storefront of the Masonic Temple as one could be while still in the same building. Originally we had just two full-time staff members working in the 700-square-foot backroom, but by 2020 there were seven of us in the space. We signed the Annex lease in late February, planning to renovate and move in by May.

Then the world fell apart. The months that followed were defined by anxiety over the virus's scale, learning social distancing norms, managing delays in manufacturing and adjusted pub dates. I worked from my dining room table as we ran everything from home. But at the end of each strange day—and on many weekends—I went to 200 Ezell. We went to view the slowly changing layout and to paint the walls. Some days, to build furniture and lay carpet tiles. These simple tasks made a chaotic world make sense. Furnishings that should have taken days to arrive took months. I tried to remember to stand six feet away from contractors and installation specialists.

On a rainy Friday in May we moved the books over to fill our new wall-to-wall shelves, and I was struck by the realization that it was really happening: in one of the strangest years we will all ever witness, we managed to build a safe new home for Hub City Press's future, full of afternoon light.

*Facing page:
Jacque Lancaster
at work proofing a
manuscript*

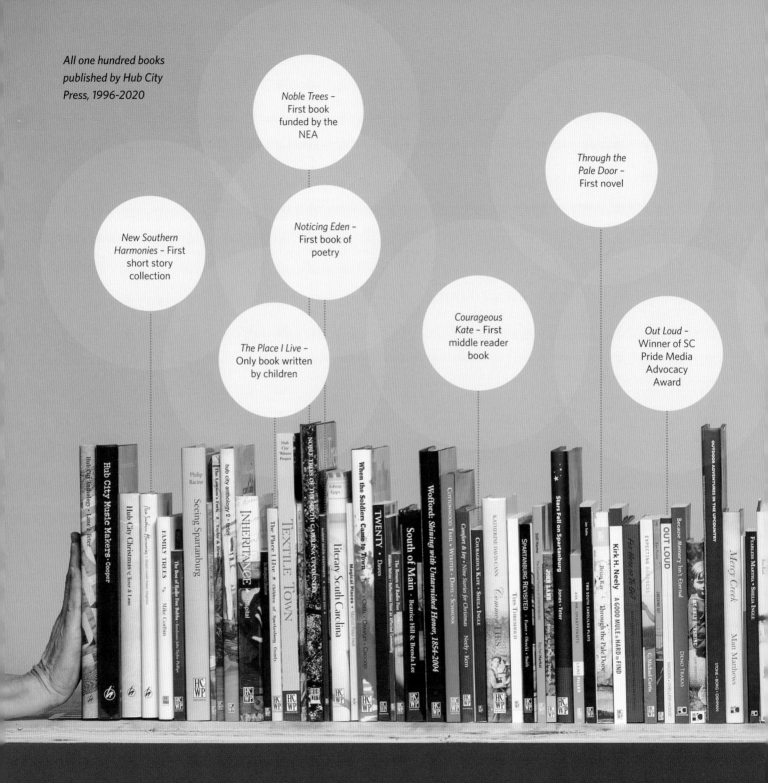

All one hundred books published by Hub City Press, 1996-2020

Noble Trees – First book funded by the NEA

Through the Pale Door – First novel

New Southern Harmonies – First short story collection

Noticing Eden – First book of poetry

The Place I Live – Only book written by children

Courageous Kate – First middle reader book

Out Loud – Winner of SC Pride Media Advocacy Award

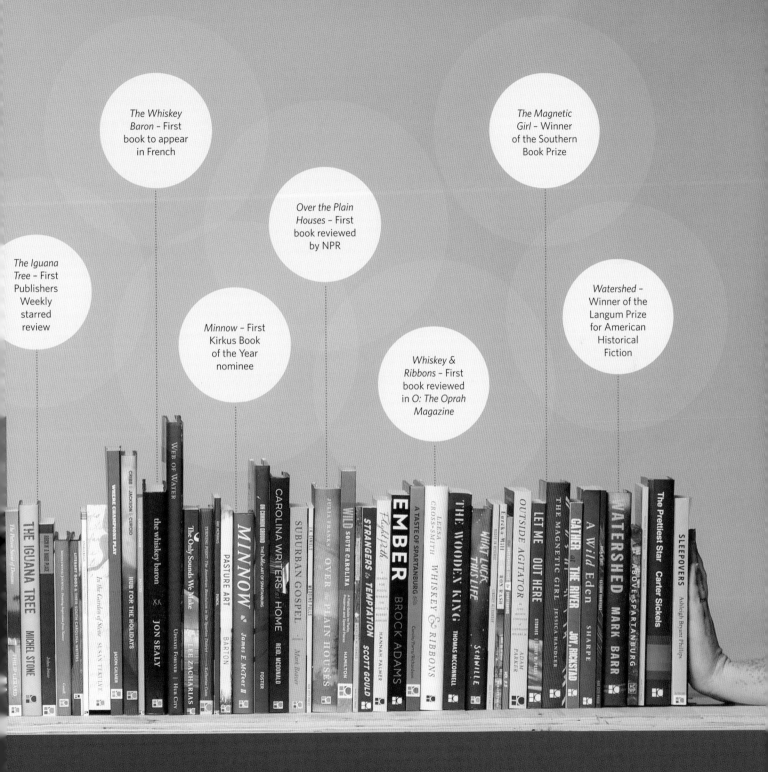

The Whiskey Baron – First book to appear in French

The Magnetic Girl – Winner of the Southern Book Prize

Over the Plain Houses – First book reviewed by NPR

The Iguana Tree – First Publishers Weekly starred review

Minnow – First Kirkus Book of the Year nominee

Watershed – Winner of the Langum Prize for American Historical Fiction

Whiskey & Ribbons – First book reviewed in *O: The Oprah Magazine*

CONTRIBUTORS

Born to a family of preachers, singers, shrinks, and teachers, **Meg Barnhouse** was born in Philadelphia and raised in the Carolinas. Married to Kiya Heartwood, they live in Austin with three cats. Mother of two grown sons, Nana to three grandchildren, Senior Minister at the UU Church of Austin, she is never bored, and never ceases to be lovingly amazed at human courage, perseverance, weakness, and hope. Her aim is to speak the truth in sermons, songs, and stories.

Marshall Chapman was the first woman to front a rock and roll band, back when women weren't yet picking up electric guitars. She's a recording artist, actress, author, and songwriter (her songs have been recorded by everybody from Emmylou Harris and Jimmy Buffett to Joe Cocker and Irma Thomas). Her fourteenth album—*Songs I Can't Live Without*—was released in April 2020.

Peter Cooper is an author, a senior lecturer at Vanderbilt University, and a Grammy-nominated musician in Nashville where he works as the Country Music Hall of Fame and Museum's senior director, writer, and producer. He is the author of *Hub City Music Makers: One Southern Town's Popular Music Legacy*.

Kerry Ferguson is a poet, playwright, and Wofford College theatre professor who has recently turned her sights to the craft of picture book writing. Her time working at Hub City Writers Project and then HUB-BUB inspired a deep love for and appreciation of our hyper-creative Spartanburg community.

Sara June Goldstein, who received the prestigious Governor's Award in the Humanities in 2018, was Literary Arts Director and Senior Coordinator of Statewide Partnerships at the South Carolina Arts Commission until her retirement in 2019 after thirty years at the agency. She is Executive Director of the Write to Change Foundation, founded in 1994 to support youth in South Carolina and beyond who use literacy and the arts to encourage social change and equity.

Jessica Handler is the author of *The Magnetic Girl*, the memoir *Invisible Sisters*, and the craft guide *Braving the Fire: A Guide to Writing About Grief and Loss*. Her writing has appeared on NPR, in *Tin House, Drunken Boat, The Bitter Southerner, Newsweek*, and *The Washington Post*. She teaches creative writing at Oglethorpe University in Atlanta and lectures internationally on writing.

Gary Henderson is a Spartanburg native and a founder of the Hub City Writers Project. He is an award-winning journalist and former South Carolina Journalist of the Year. He was a staff writer for both the Spartanburg *Herald-Journal* and the *Spartanburg Journal*. Gary is retired and lives in Costa Rica.

Originally from New York, **Eric Kocher** moved to Spartanburg in 2011 to serve as a Writer-in-Residence for the Hub City Writers Project after receiving his MFA in Creative Writing from the University of Houston. Before joining the Spartanburg marketing firm ALINE, he worked with HUB-BUB and the Chapman Cultural

Center where he managed public art projects and programs. Some of his writing has appeared in *Boston Review*, *Best New Poets*, *A Public Space*, and elsewhere.

John Lane is—with his wife, Betsy Teter, and good friend, Gary Henderson—one of the three founders of the Hub City Writers Project. He taught for thirty-two years in English and environmental studies at Wofford College and in his long career has published eighteen books of poetry, nonfiction, and fiction.

Jameelah Lang's work has recently appeared or is forthcoming in national literary magazines such as the *Michigan Quarterly Review*, *The Cincinnati Review*, *The Kenyon Review*, and more. Her writing has received competitive awards and recognition from the Bread Loaf Writers' Conference, Sewanee Writers' Conference, the Virginia Center for Creative Arts, and the Vermont Studio. She is an Assistant Teaching Professor at Rockhurst University and serves on the board for the Radius of Arab-American Writers.

Kari Jackson Mailloux was Assistant Director at the Hub City Writers Project from 2010 to 2013 after receiving her MFA in Creative Writing from the University of Kansas. At Hub City, she helped open the Bookshop, co-founded the Expecting Goodness Short Film Festival, and edited or designed five books. She now lives in her hometown of Hutchinson, Kansas, where she is Director of Strategic Initiatives at Hutchinson Community Foundation, wife to Phillip, and mom to Jackson, Paige, and Sydney.

Thomas McConnell forded the Tugaloo River for South Carolina twenty years ago to teach literature and writing at USC Upstate. He's found Spartanburg a good place for words and reckons he's written perhaps a million of them in that time. Around a hundred thousand have actually been published. He is the author of *The Wooden King*.

Rob McDonald is a photographer who has been living a double life as an English professor and Associate Dean of the Faculty at the Virginia Military Institute for a number of years. He has won fellowships from the Virginia Museum of Fine Arts (2019) and the Virginia Center for the Creative Arts (2014). His books include *Cy's Rollei* (with Sally Mann), *Carolina Writers at Home*, and most recently, *The Father Box* (with John Lane). Rob is a native of rural Marion County, South Carolina, which he still considers home.

Kate McMullen is the assistant director of Hub City Press. She grew up in Greensboro, North Carolina, and received her MFA in fiction from the University of North Carolina at Wilmington. Her fiction has appeared in *Paper Darts*, *The Boiler*, *Foglifter*, and *The Pinch*.

Kirk H. Neely is a native of Spartanburg and the oldest of eight children. He grew up working at the family business, Neely Lumber Company. He was educated at Furman University, Southern Seminary, and Harvard Divinity School. Kirk and his wife, Clare, have been married since 1966. They are parents of five children and have thirteen grandchildren. Kirk is a storyteller, a freelance writer, a teacher, a pastoral counselor, and a retired pastor.

Thomas Pierce is the author of a novel, *The Afterlives*, and a collection of stories, *Hall of Small Mammals*, for which he was honored with the National Book Foundation's 5 Under 35 Award. He's published stories in *The New Yorker*, *The Atlantic Monthly*, and elsewhere. He holds an MFA from the University of Virginia, where he was a Poe/Faulkner Fellow.

Brenda Lee Pryce is a retired South Carolina State Representative, author, community historian, and community activist. She is married to Caveril Pryce of Jamaica, West Indies, and they have one cat, Buddy.

Meg Reid is the Director of Hub City Press. Raised in the far reaches of the Northeast, she moved South to pursue an MFA in Nonfiction from University of North Carolina Wilmington and then to Spartanburg a few years later to work for Hub City, where she found her literary home. She is both a book designer and an editor and writes extensively about all areas of design. She lives in a bungalow in Hampton Heights with her husband and dog.

Bobbie Jean Shepard is an English teacher and writer living in Spartanburg with her husband and two sons. She grew up on a horse farm in the foothills and has always enjoyed being outdoors. She spends her free time running, hiking with her family, and writing poetry or reading. Her poetry has appeared in *Emrys Journal* and *The Stillwater Review*.

George Singleton has published eight collections of stories, two novels, and a book of writing advice. A member of the Fellowship of Southern Writers and John C. Cobb Endowed Professor in the Humanities at Wofford College, his Selected Stories, *You Want More*, was published in fall 2020 by Hub City Press.

A 2019 National Poetry Series Finalist, **Leslie Sainz**'s work has appeared in or is forthcoming from *AGNI, jubilat, Narrative, Black Warrior Review, Ninth Letter*, and others. She's received scholarships, fellowships, and residencies from CantoMundo, The Miami Writers Institute, *The Adroit Journal*, the Hub City Writers Project, and the Stadler Center

for Poetry at Bucknell University. She works as the Outreach Manager for the Hub City Writers Project.

Kathryn Schwille is the author of the novel, *What Luck, This Life*, named by the *Atlanta Journal-Constitution* as one of the best Southern books of 2018. She lives in Charlotte, where she teaches and mentors writers at Charlotte Center for Literary Arts.

Emily Louise Smith is an assistant professor of creative writing at the University of North Carolina Wilmington, where she directs The Publishing Laboratory and teaches publishing arts. She also serves as publisher of the award-winning sister entities *Ecotone* magazine and literary imprint Lookout Books, which she co-founded. Her writing—on the art of publishing, teaching, running, motherhood, and place, among other subjects—appears in *Outside, House Method*, the *Southern Review*, and *Literary Publishing in the Twenty-First Century*.

Brad Steinecke is a Spartanburg native who has been captivated by local history and culture for the past two decades. Since 2009, he has worked in the Kennedy Room of the Spartanburg County Public Libraries, where he assists researchers, curates exhibits, and delivers local history presentations. Brad also serves on the city's Historic Architecture Review Board and boards of the Hub City Writers Project, the Tyger River Foundation, and the Hampton Heights Neighborhood Association.

Michel Stone has published a couple of novels and a dozen or so essays and stories. She's had too many cool literary experiences to rank her top five moments since Hub City Press published her first novel in 2012, but a mention in *The New Yorker* and giving a major university's commencement address rank way up there. She and her husband Eliot will celebrate their twenty-fifth anniversary this year, and she is most proud of their three marvelous children. Michel is close to finishing the first draft of a novel she has tinkered with for nearly a decade ... she hopes.

David Taylor is an Assistant Professor of Environmental Humanities in the Sustainability Studies Program housed in the School of Marine and Atmospheric Sciences at Stony Brook University. His writing crosses disciplinary boundaries and genres—scholarship, science/technical writing, creative nonfiction, and poetry. However, always at the core of his work is an interest in and concern for environmental sustainability and community. He is the author and editor of nine books and remembers fondly of his days paddling on Lawson's Fork.

Susan Tekulve's newest book is *Second Shift: Essays*. She is the author of *In the Garden of Stone*, winner of the 2012 South Carolina First Novel Prize and a 2014 Gold IPPY Award. She's also published two short story collections: *Savage Pilgrims* and *My Mother's War Stories*. Her short stories and essays have appeared in journals such as *Denver Quarterly*, *The Georgia Review*, *The Louisville Review*, *New Letters*, and *Shenandoah*.

Betsy Teter served as executive director of the Hub City Writers Project for twenty-two years, editing books, corralling writers, balancing the checkbook, dreaming big, raising money, harassing book reviewers, running board meetings, hauling heavy boxes, writing grants, and saying Bravo! a lot. She hopes the new generation at Hub City will let her hang around for decades to come.

G.C. Waldrep's most recent books are *feast gently* (Tupelo, 2018), winner of the William Carlos Williams Award from the Poetry Society of America, and the long poem *Testament* (BOA Editions, 2015). He is also the author of *Southern Workers and the Search for Community: Spartanburg County, S.C., 1880-1950* (Illinois, 2000). Waldrep lives in Lewisburg, Pennsylvania, where he teaches creative writing at Bucknell University and edits the journal *West Branch*.

A native of Little Rock, Arkansas, **Anne Waters** has worked in bookselling and publishing for more than thirty years. She has served as the executive director of the Hub City Writers Project since 2017. Her pastimes (besides reading) include teaching and practicing yoga, making imperfect ceramic pots, cooking, and gardening. She and her husband, Andrew, and their son, Eli, love to travel.

Board members Betsy Richardson (left) and Marjorie Boafo-Appiah (facing page) prepare for Delicious Reads 2019.

OUR BOARD

Since the Hub City Writers Project became a non-profit organization in 1997, its board has played a pivotal role in the success of the organization. Founding board chair Winston Hardegree, a writer and retired business executive, led a team of volunteers committed to the idea that literature could be a powerful tool for building community. That board set a standard for servant-leadership that persists to this day. There's an old adage that non-profit board members contribute their time, talent, and treasure to serve the organization, and that's been true for our organization. Hub City board members have never been figureheads. They are hands-on leaders. They deliver hundreds of donor books each fall, sign and stuff fundraising letters, and even make beds for the faculty at the Writing in Place conference. They host visiting writers overnight and proofread manuscripts. They assemble furniture for the bookstore, tend bar at events, bake cakes, arrange flowers, and write checks for regular operations and special projects. Board members partner with the staff to solve problems and develop new initiatives. The Hub City board remains dedicated to our mission of cultivating readers and nurturing writers, and we look forward to the next twenty-five years.

Melissa Walker
Board member, 2004-2012 and 2013-2020
Board president, 2007-2008

2020 Board Members

Marjorie Boafo-Appiah
Michele Cook
Haidee Courson
John Cribb
Ed Epps
Latria Graham
Frances Hardy
Araceli Hernandez-Laroche
Ralph Hilsman
John Lane, Emeritus

Byron Morris
Susan Myers
Dwight Patterson, Emeritus
Betsy Richardson
Chris Smutzer
Sally Spencer
Brad Steinecke
Jenny Stevens
Betsy Teter, Emeritus
Diane Vecchio

OUR VOLUNTEERS

On Monday, Bea Bruce updates our *New York Times* bestseller lists. On Tuesday, Nancy Kenney puts out new releases. On Wednesday, Byron Morris buys a few of the books Nancy put out and draws our customers into conversation with his unmistakable Mississippi drawl. Every other Thursday Ned Barrett steps away from his duties at Partners for Active Living to volunteer, which he has done since we opened. Alternating Thursdays you will meet Wendy King, the most voracious reader in our midst. (And we read a lot.) And on alternating Fridays, Christina Johanningmeier and Carol Epps will warmly welcome you. Our volunteers make our bookshop a true community bookstore. They are unflagging in their support and unwavering in their commitment. And we adore them.

Jan Scalisi, in memoriam

Nancy Kenney

HUB CITY AUTHORS, 1996 – 2020

A

Brock Adams, *Ember* (2017)

Anjail Rashida Ahmad, *Home is Where: An Anthology of African American Poetry from the Carolinas* (2011)

Dan Albergotti, *Carolina Writers at Home* (2015)

Lindsey Alexander, *Rodeo in Reverse* (2018)

Paul Allen, *Twenty: South Carolina Poetry Fellows* (2005)

William Allen, *Hub City Anthology 2* (2000)

Acecily Alexander, *Home is Where: An Anthology of African American Poetry from the Carolinas* (2011)

Marcus Amaker, *Home is Where: An Anthology of African American Poetry from the Carolinas* (2011)

C. Mack Amick, *Hub City Christmas* (1997)
Stars Fell on Spartanburg (2008)

Shirlette Ammons, *Home is Where: An Anthology of African American Poetry from the Carolinas* (2011)

Alvin "Little Pink" Anderson, *Stars Fell on Spartanburg* (2008)

B

Jan Bailey, *Twenty: South Carolina Poetry Fellows* (2005)

Anne Alexander Bain, *Hub City Christmas* (1997)

Ross K. Baker, *Textile Town* (2002)

Meg Barnhouse, *Hub City Anthology* (1996)
Hub City Christmas (1997)
The Best of Radio Free Bubba (1998)
In Morgan's Shadow (2001)
Return of Radio Free Bubba (2005)
The Hub City Writers Project: The First 25 Years (2020)

Mark Barr, *Watershed* (2019)

Ned Barrett, *Outdoor Adventures in the Upcountry* (2010)

Marlin Barton, *Pasture Art* (2015)

Natalie Baszile, *Gather at the River: 25 Authors on Fishing* (2019)

Joseph Bathanti, *Carolina Writers at Home* (2015)

Mark Beaver, *Suburban Gospel* (2016)

Philip Belcher, *Still Home: The Essential Poetry of Spartanburg* (2008)

Patricia Benton, *Inheritance: Selections from the South Carolina Fiction Project* (2001)

Linda Powers Bilanchone, *Hub City Christmas* (1997)

Frank Bill, *Gather at the River: 25 Authors on Fishing* (2019)

Elise Blackwell, *Literary Dogs & Their South Carolina Writers* (2012)

Tom Blagden, *Web of Water* (2014)

Doyle Boggs, *Textile Town* (2002)
When the Soldiers Came to Town (2004)
Wofford: Shining with Untarnished Honor (2005)

Cynthia Boiter, *Inheritance: Selections from the South Carolina Fiction Project* (2001)
Hub for the Holidays: Spartanburg Writers on Christmas (2013)

Clay Bolt, *Web of Water* (2014)

Ted Borg, *Outdoor Adventures in the Upcountry* (2010)

Robert Botsch, *Textile Town* (2002)

Bob Bourguignon, *Hub for the Holidays: Spartanburg Writers on Christmas* (2013)

Cathy Smith Bowers, *Twenty: South Carolina Poetry Fellows* (2005)
Hidden Voices: Reflections from an Affected Community (2005)

C.J. Box, *Gather at the River: 25 Authors on Fishing* (2019)

William Boyle, *Gather at the River: 25 Authors on Fishing* (2019)

Kathryn Brackett, *Expecting Goodness & Other Stories* (2009)

Kavin Bradner, *Above Spartanburg* (2019)

Earl Braggs, *Home is Where: An Anthology of African American Poetry from the Carolinas* (2011)

Don Bramblett, *Stars Fell on Spartanburg* (2008)

JoAnn Mitchell Brasington, *Textile Town* (2002)
Wofford: Shining with Untarnished Honor (2005)

Butler Brewton, *Hub City Anthology* (1996)
Hub City Christmas (1997)

Still Home: The Essential Poetry of Spartanburg (2008)

Stars Fell on Spartanburg (2008)

Home is Where: An Anthology of African American Poetry from the Carolinas (2011)

Glenn Bridges, *Textile Town* (2002)

Hunter Bridges, *Outdoor Adventures in the Upcountry* (2010)

John W. Brinsfield, *When the Soldiers Came to Town* (2004)

Linda Beatrice Brown, *Home is Where: An Anthology of African American Poetry from the Carolinas* (2011)

Rob Brown, *In Morgan's Shadow* (2001)
Outdoor Adventures in the Upcountry (2010)
Hub for the Holidays: Spartanburg Writers on Christmas (2013)

Taylor Brown, *Gather at the River: 25 Authors on Fishing* (2019)

Alan Buie, *Textile Town* (2002)

Jessica Bundschuh, *Twenty: South Carolina Poetry Fellows* (2005)

Christopher Bundy, *Stars Fell on Spartanburg* (2008)
Expecting Goodness & Other Stories (2009)

Russ Burns, *Outdoor Adventures in the Upcountry* (2010)

David J. Burt, *Inheritance: Selections from the South Carolina Fiction Project* (2001)

Judy Burke Bynum, *Stars Fell on Spartanburg* (2008)

Kathryn Stripling Byer, *Carolina Writers at Home* (2015)

C

Alice Cabiness, *Inheritance: Selections from the South Carolina Fiction Project* (2001)

Christian Campbell, *Home is Where: An Anthology of African American Poetry from the Carolinas* (2011)

Katherine Davis Cann, *Textile Town* (2002)
When the Soldiers Came to Town (2004)
Turning Point: The American Revolution in the Spartan District (2014)

David L. Carlton, *Hub City Anthology 2* (2000)
Textile Town (2002)

Robin Ely Carroll, *Hub City Christmas* (1997)

Skip Eisiminger, *Outdoor Adventures in the Upcountry* (2010)

Edward Emory: *Artists Among Us: 100 Faces of Art in Spartanburg* (2011)

Edwin C. Epps, *Literary South Carolina* (2004)
Still Home: The Essential Poetry of Spartanburg (2008)
Stars Fell on Spartanburg (2008)
Hub for the Holidays: Spartanburg Writers on Christmas (2013)

Bill Epton, *Stars Fell on Spartanburg* (2008)

Percival Everett, *Home is Where: An Anthology of African American Poetry from the Carolinas* (2011)

F

John Faris Jr., *Outdoor Adventures in the Upcountry* (2010)

Peter Fennell, *Inheritance: Selections from the South Carolina Fiction Project* (2001)

Randolph C. Ferebee, *Hub for the Holidays: Spartanburg Writers on Christmas* (2013)

Elaine Lang Ferguson, *Hub City Christmas* (1997)

Kerry Ferguson, *The Hub City Writers Project: The First 25 Years* (2020)

Linda Ferguson, *Twenty: South Carolina Poetry Fellows* (2005)

Terry A. Ferguson, *Textile Town* (2002)

Lane Filler, *Ask Mr. Smartypants* (2008)

Malinda Fillingim, *Hub for the Holidays: Spartanburg Writers on Christmas* (2013)

Nikkey Finney, *Home is Where: An Anthology of African American Poetry from the Carolinas* (2011)
Carolina Writers at Home (2015)

Keith Flynn, *Carolina Writers at Home* (2015)

Starkey Flythe, *Twenty: South Carolina Poetry Fellows* (2005)

Olivia Heffner Fortson, *Stars Fell on Spartanburg* (2008)

Carroll Foster, *Spartanburg Revisited* (2007)
For Here or to Go: Spartanburg's Drive-ins, Drive-Thrus, and Diners (2009)
On Common Ground: The Public Art of Spartanburg (2015)

Lib Willis Fowler, *Stars Fell on Spartanburg* (2008)

John Fowler, *Textile Town* (2002)

Dorothea Benton Frank, *Literary Dogs & Their South Carolina Writers* (2012)

Julia Franks, *Over the Plain Houses* (2016)

Mindy Friddle, *Literary Dogs & Their South Carolina Writers* (2012)

G

Frye Gaillard, *Hub City Music Makers* (1997)

Phillip Gardner, *Inheritance: Selections from the South Carolina Fiction Project* (2001)

Nichole Gause, *Home is Where: An Anthology of African American Poetry from the Carolinas* (2011)

Marcel Gauthier, *Still Home: The Essential Poetry of Spartanburg* (2008)

Christopher George, *Hub for the Holidays: Spartanburg Writers on Christmas* (2013)

Philip Gerard, *The Patron Saint of Dreams* (2012)

David Gessner, *Carolina Writers at Home* (2015)

Andrew Geyer, *Literary Dogs & Their South Carolina Writers* (2012)

Jason Gilmer, *Where Champions Play* (2013)

Ernest Glenn, *Outdoor Adventures in the Upcountry* (2010)

Peter Godfrey, *Outdoor Adventures in the Upcountry* (2010)

Cecile Hanna Goding, *Inheritance: Selections from the South Carolina Fiction Project* (2001)

Rebecca T. Godwin, *Inheritance: Selections from the South Carolina Fiction Project* (2001)

Max Goldberg, *Hub City Anthology* (1996)

Sara June Goldstein, *The Hub City Writers Project: The First 25 Years* (2020)

Aly Goodwin, *Still Home: The Essential Poetry of Spartanburg* (2008)

Scott Gould, *New Southern Harmonies* (1998)
Outdoor Adventures in the Upcountry (2010)
Strangers to Temptation (2017)
Gather at the River: 25 Authors on Fishing (2019)

Jaki Shelton Green, *Home is Where: An Anthology of African American Poetry from the Carolinas* (2011)

Allan Gurganus, *Carolina Writers at Home* (2015)

H

Erin Haire, *Hub for the Holidays: Spartanburg Writers on Christmas* (2013)

Ed Y. Hall, *Stars Fell on Spartanburg* (2008)

Liesel Hamilton, *Wild South Carolina* (2016)

Susan Hamilton, *Wild South Carolina* (2016)

Tanya Bordeaux Hamm, *Textile Town* (2002)

Jessica Handler, *The Magnetic Girl* (2019)
The Hub City Writers Project: The First 25 Years (2020)

Frances Hardy, *Hub City Anthology* (1996)
Still Home: The Essential Poetry of Spartanburg (2008)

Winston Hardegree, *Hub City Anthology* (1996)

Beth Webb Hart, *Literary Dogs & Their South Carolina Writers* (2012)

Terrence Hayes, *Home is Where: An Anthology of African American Poetry from the Carolinas* (2011)

Tommy Hayes, *Literary Dogs & Their South Carolina Writers* (2012)

Shelby Hearon, *New Southern Harmonies* (1998)

Rachel Heath, *Home is Where: An Anthology of African American Poetry from the Carolinas* (2011)

Robert Heaton, *Inheritance: Selections from the South Carolina Fiction Project* (2001)

Mike Hembree, *Hub City Christmas* (1997)
The Seasons of Harold Hatcher (2000)
Textile Town (2002)
Stars Fell on Spartanburg (2008)

Rachel Harkai, *Still Home: The Essential Poetry of Spartanburg* (2008)
Apartment D: Five Years of Writers in Residence (2011)

Alice Hatcher Henderson, *Textile Town* (2002)

Lilah Hegnauer, *Pantry* (2014)

Gary Henderson, *Hub City Anthology* (1996)
Hub City Christmas (1997)
The Lawson's Fork: Headwaters to Confluence (2000)
Textile Town (2002)
Stars Fell on Spartanburg (2008)
The Hub City Writers Project: The First 25 Years (2020)

Marc Henderson, *Hub City Christmas* (1997)

Meg Reid, *Carolina Writers at Home* (2015)
   The Hub City Writers Project: The First 25 Years (2020)

Tracy J. Revels, *Wofford: Shining with Untarnished Honor* (2005)

S. Paul Rice, *Inheritance: Selections from the South Carolina Fiction Project* (2001)
   Twenty: South Carolina Poetry Fellows (2005)

Alex Richardson, *Still Home: The Essential Poetry of Spartanburg* (2008)
   Stars Fell on Spartanburg (2008)

Amanda Richardson, *A Taste of Spartanburg* (2017)

Lisa Caston Richie, *Textile Town* (2002)

Eric Rickstad, *Gather at the River: 25 Authors on Fishing* (2019)

Elisabeth Robe, *Hub City Anthology 2* (2000)
   Stars Fell on Spartanburg (2008)

Pat Robertson, *Outdoor Adventures in the Upcountry* (2010)

Bertice Teague Robinson, *Hub for the Holidays: Spartanburg Writers on Christmas* (2013)

Esteban Rodriguez, *Dusk & Dust* (2019)

Joyce M. Rose-Harris, *Home is Where: An Anthology of African American Poetry from the Carolinas* (2011)

S

Leslie Sainz, *The Hub City Writers Project: The First 25 Years* (2020)

William H. Sapp, *When the Soldiers Came to Town* (2004)

Dori Sanders, *Family Trees* (1998)

J.C. Sasser, *Gather at the River: 25 Authors on Fishing* (2019)

Catherine Robe Schumacher, *Hub for the Holidays: Spartanburg Writers on Christmas* (2013)

Peter Schmunk, *Cottonwood Trail* (2006)

Kathryn Schwille, *What Luck, This Life* (2018)
   The Hub City Writers Project: The First 25 Years (2020)

J. Todd Scott, *Gather at the River: 25 Authors on Fishing* (2019)

James Scott, *Hub City Anthology 2* (2000)

Jon Sealy, *The Whiskey Baron* (2014)

Nicole Seitz, *Literary Dogs & Their South Carolina Writers* (2012)

Phillip Shabazz, *Home is Where: An Anthology of African American Poetry from the Carolinas* (2011)

K.I.N.G. Shakur, *Home is Where: An Anthology of African American Poetry from the Carolinas* (2011)

Rosa Shand, *Hub City Anthology* (1997)
   Hub City Christmas (1997)
   New Southern Harmonies (1998)
   Inheritance: Selections from the South Carolina Fiction Project (2001)
   In Morgan's Shadow (2001)
   Expecting Goodness & Other Stories (2009)

Ruth Shanor, *Hub City Christmas* (1997)

Scott Sharpe, *A Wild Eden* (2019)

Danny Shelton, *Textile Town* (2002)

Bobbie Jean Shepard, *The Hub City Writers Project: The First 25 Years* (2020)

Evie Shockley, *Home is Where: An Anthology of African American Poetry from the Carolinas* (2011)

Pamela Burgess Shucker, *Outdoor Adventures in the Upcountry* (2010)

Carter Sickels, *The Prettiest Star* (2020)

George Singleton, *New Southern Harmonies* (1998)
   Literary Dogs & Their South Carolina Writers (2012)
   Carolina Writers at Home (2015)
   You Want More (2020)
   The Hub City Writers Project: The First 25 Years (2020)

Susan Sistare, *Hub for the Holidays: Spartanburg Writers on Christmas* (2013)

Warren Slesinger, *Twenty: South Carolina Poetry Fellows* (2005)

Alexander Smalls, *Hub City Anthology 2* (2000)

Emily Smith, *Still Home: The Essential Poetry of Spartanburg* (2008)

Emily Louise Smith, *Spartanburg Revisited* (2007)
   Apartment D: Five Years of Writers in Residence (2011)
   The Hub City Writers Project: The First 25 Years (2020)

Michael Farris Smith, *Gather at the River: 25 Authors on Fishing* (2019)

Cooper Smith, *Hub City Anthology* (1996)
   Hub City Christmas (1997)

Kay Smithford, *Hub City Anthology 2* (2000)

Betty Burgin Snow, *Expecting Goodness & Other Stories* (2009)

Charles Henry Sowell, *Outdoor Adventures in the Upcountry* (2010)

Sandy Staggs, *Stars Fell on Spartanburg* (2008)

Melody Starkey, *Inheritance: Selections from the South Carolina Fiction Project* (2001)

Brad Steinecke, *Stars Fell on Spartanburg* (2008)
   The Hub City Writers Project: The First 25 Years (2020)

John Stevenson, *Hub City Anthology* (1996)

Tori Steyne, *Wild South Carolina* (2016)

Shandi Stevenson, *Outdoor Adventures in the Upcountry* (2010)

Stephen Stinson, *Artists Among Us: 100 Faces of Art in Spartanburg* (2011)

Allen Stokes, *Textile Town* (2002)

Philip Stone, *Textile Town* (2002)
   When the Soldiers Came to Town (2004)
   Wofford: Shining with Untarnished Honor (2005)
   Stars Fell on Spartanburg (2008)

Tammy Stokes, *Stars Fell on Spartanburg* (2008)

Michel Stone, *Stars Fell on Spartanburg* (2008)
   Expecting Goodness & Other Stories (2009)
   Outdoor Adventures in the Upcountry (2010)
   The Iguana Tree (2012)
   The Hub City Writers Project: The First 25 Years (2020)

Erik Storey, *Gather at the River: 25 Authors on Fishing* (2019)

Sharan Strange, *Home is Where: An Anthology of African American Poetry from the Carolinas* (2011)

Rodger E. Stroup, *Wofford: Shining with Untarnished Honor* (2005)

Stephanie T. Suell, *Home is Where: An Anthology of African American Poetry from the Carolinas* (2011)

Christine Swager, *Come to the Cowpens* (2002)

Mike Rice Swain, *Stars Fell on Spartanburg* (2008)

T

Bob Talbert, *Hub City Anthology* (1996)

James Talley, *Stars Fell on Spartanburg* (2008)

Bill Taylor, *The Lawson's Fork, Headwaters to Confluence* (2000)

David Taylor, *Hub City Anthology* (1996)
The Lawson's Fork: Headwaters to Confluence (2000)
The Hub City Writers Project: The First 25 Years (2020)

Kim Taylor, *The Best of Radio Free Bubba* (1998)
Return of Radio Free Bubba (2005)

Matthew Teague, *Hub City Christmas* (1997)

Gerald Teaster, *Outdoor Adventures in the Upcountry* (2010)

Susan Tekulve, *Expecting Goodness & Other Stories* (2009)
In the Garden of Stone (2013)
The Hub City Writers Project: The First 25 Years (2020)

Betsy Wakefield Teter, *Hub City Anthology* (1996)
Hub City Christmas (1997)
Hub City Anthology 2 (2000)
Textile Town (2002)
Stars Fell on Spartanburg (2008)
Literary Dogs & Their South Carolina Writers (2012)
The Hub City Writers Project: The First 25 Years (2020)

Joni Tevis, *Outdoor Adventures in the Upcountry* (2010)

P.L. Thomas, *Still Home: The Essential Poetry of Spartanburg* (2008)

Fred Thompson III, *Inheritance: Selections from the South Carolina Fiction Project* (2001)

Susan Thoms, *When the Soldiers Came to Town* (2004)

Ingrid Throft, *Gather at the River: 25 Authors on Fishing* (2019)

Gerald Thurmond, *Hub City Anthology 2* (2000)
Stars Fell on Spartanburg (2008)
Outdoor Adventures in the Upcountry (2010)

David Tillinghast, *Inheritance: Selections from the South Carolina Fiction Project* (2001)

Cedric Tillman, *Home is Where: An Anthology of African American Poetry from the Carolinas* (2011)

Deno Trakas, *Hub City Anthology* (1996)
Hub City Christmas (1997)
New Southern Harmonies (1998)
Inheritance: Selections from the South Carolina Fiction Project (2001)
In Morgan's Shadow (2001)
Wofford: *Shining with Untarnished Honor* (2005)
Still Home: The Essential Poetry of Spartanburg (2008)
Stars Fell on Spartanburg (2008)
Expecting Goodness & Other Stories (2009)
Because Memory Isn't Eternal (2010)

Daniel Cross Turner, *Hub for the Holidays: Spartanburg Writers on Christmas* (2013)

Susan Turpin, *When the Soldiers Came to Town* (2004)

Jon Tuttle, *Two South Carolina Plays* (2009)

U

Gloria Underwood, *Hub City Christmas* (1997)

V

Diane Vecchio, *Textile Town* (2002)

W

G.C. Waldrep III, *Textile Town* (2002)
The Hub City Writers Project: The First 25 Years (2020)

Evelyn Brock Waldrop, *Hub City Christmas* (1997)

Melissa Walker, *When the Soldiers Came to Town* (2004)

Daniel Wallace, *Carolina Writers at Home* (2015)

M.O. Walsh, *Gather at the River: 25 Authors on Fishing* (2019)

Winnie Walsh, *Stars Fell on Spartanburg* (2008)

Kimberly Ward, *This Threshold: Writing on the End of Life* (2007)

Anne Waters, *The Hub City Writers Project: The First 25 Years* (2020)

Mary Chapman Webster, *Hub City Anthology 2* (2000)

Thomas Webster, *Textile Town* (2002)
Cottonwood Trail (2006)

Ceille Baird Welch, *Inheritance: Selections from the South Carolina Fiction Project* (2001)

Marjorie Heath Wentworth, *Noticing Eden* (2003)
Literary Dogs & Their South Carolina Writers (2012)

Kathleen Whitten, *Twenty: South Carolina Poetry Fellows* (2005)

Patrick Whitfill, *Apartment D: Five Years of Writers in Residence* (2011)

Carolyn Beard Whitlow, *Home is Where: An Anthology of African American Poetry from the Carolinas* (2011)

Candace Wiley, *Home is Where: An Anthology of African American Poetry from the Carolinas* (2011)

Greg Williams, *Inheritance: Selections from the South Carolina Fiction Project* (2001)

JP Williams, *Hub for the Holidays: Spartanburg Writers on Christmas* (2013)

Cynthia Reid Willis, *Hub City Anthology 2* (2000)

Dick Willis, *Hub for the Holidays: Spartanburg Writers on Christmas* (2013)

Jeffrey R. Willis, *Hub City Anthology 2* (2000)
Textile Town (2002)
When the Soldiers Came to Town (2004)

Stephen Willis, *Hub for the Holidays: Spartanburg Writers on Christmas* (2013)

Roger Wilkie, *When the Soldiers Came to Town* (2004)

Roy Wilson, *Stars Fell on Spartanburg* (2008)

Y

Jeffrey Young, *For Here or to Go: Spartanburg's Drive-ins, Drive-Thrus, and Diners* (2009)

Z

Lee Zacharias, *The Only Sounds We Make* (2014)

Susan Jackson Zurenda, *Inheritance: Selections from the South Carolina Fiction Project* (2001)
In Morgan's Shadow (2001)
Stars Fell on Spartanburg (2008)

Not included in this list (for space reasons!): Additional contributors to the books *Wofford: Shining with Untarnished Honor, The Place I Live, Artists Among Us, On Common Ground,* and *A Taste of Spartanburg.*

HUB CITY PRESS

Hub City Press is an independent press in Spartanburg, South Carolina, that publishes well-crafted, high-quality works by new and established authors, with an emphasis on the Southern experience. We are committed to high-caliber novels, short stories, poetry, plays, memoir, and works emphasizing regional culture and history. We are particularly interested in books with a strong sense of place. Hub City Press is an imprint of the non-profit Hub City Writers Project, founded in 1995 to foster a sense of community through the literary arts. Our metaphor of organization purposely looks backward to the nineteenth century when Spartanburg was known as the "hub city," a place where railroads converged and departed.

Recent Hub City Press Titles

Sleepovers • Ashleigh Bryant Phillips

The Prettiest Star • Carter Sickels

Mustard, Milk, and Gin • Megan Denton Ray

Above Spartanburg • Kavin Bradner

Dusk & Dust • Esteban Rodriguez

Watershed • Mark Barr